Let Me Tell You What Mama Said

By Terri Elizabeth Lyons

Edited by Dr. Suzanne Cloud

978-0-6151-9314-4
Copyright year: 2008

Dedicated to the other half of my heart,
My mother, Hazel Lyons

Acknowledgements

To my mother, without whom there wouldn't be any story. With all of my love, all of our blood, thank you for being my mother.

I must thank my life long friend and sister, Linda Jordan Zabalou. You had my back from day one. This is the result of our Friday night oldies kick outs. Hot Wings!

My dear coworkers Ronald Faulk who kicked me, supported me and never had any doubt. To Sharon Szamboti-Kraus whose dancing eyes and beautiful face lit my day. You extended your hand...and your heart was in it. To Bill Hill Jr. for his insight and enthusiasm. Thank you Floyd Rudd for taking me to see Uncle Greenie.

Sue Antrim had it for me hands down from day one. I'll always be your Sweet Pea.

To the brilliant historian Harrison Ridley Junior who made time for me on the air waves and my patient editor Dr. Suzanne Cloud with her priceless guidance and criticism. To Chipo Jolibois thank you so much for your support and advice. You gave me your best. We went from coworkers to friends in the most peculiar way and you brought good vibes into my life.

To my husband, Benny who stood beside me a distance with love and patience to allow the room and time needed to learn, create and sometimes erupt. His tender arms and encouragement were always available.

The Jordan family who was especially attentive. They opened their home for me featuring my work at their book club meeting. Their love and support will always be appreciated. (Sister Renee and Mother Carol) Chocolates to you!

To Angie Mobley who happened to be there just when I needed her most.

I thank EVERYONE who helped me and supported me every step of the way.

I even thank the nay sayers who are a comfort to my feet.

I couldn't have made without any of you. I want everyone to enjoy and inspire, learn, teach and share.

11/20/07
Terri Elizabeth Lyons

Contents

By the time I came along, the backroom had
long been a bathroom. It was eerie to walk up the
long dark steps even as the hall light dimly burned
above my head. Midway up the stairs on my right
was the room. My heritage room. I used to visit
that room every time I came to the old homestead.
The wallpaper had bursts of rose buds strewn all
over with pale green and white stripes behind the
bunches of buds, but time turned the peeling paper
gold, standing in stark contrast to the fresh white
curtains hanging across the large hazy window.
The dark hardwood floors were worn and creaky.
An old dresser sat in the corner with legs as long
as mine. I came into the room and sat on the side
of the bed looking out the window. It was a view
of a lonely field that led to Sumneytown Pike. My
mother was born in that dingy room and so was her
mother. My great grandmother died in this same
room while sleeping. Haunted by spirits, I scurried
down the hall to my original destination, the
bathroom. The large room had a huge footed tub
with no shower and a large toilet with a tall filling
tank. The sink had individual spigots for hot and
cold water with a chained plug in the middle of the
lime-stained sink. A fluorescent light was on either
side of the mirror mounted high on the massive red
wall. I had to reach beyond my capacity to get the
paper roll, which was too low for a toilet that sat so

high. I was in my Sunday best; my black wool jumper and red turtleneck top. I enjoyed the reflection in the long mirror mounted on the back of the door. I stood there twisting my red and black yarn adorning my freshly straightened ponytails that had come unraveled. I hopped on the pot and had an elevated view of the desolate backyard that reached forever. The pink sliver of soap at the sink smelled of Camay clashing with my Avon Pretty Peach Cachet. I took one last peek of my picture perfect self and headed out the door.

When I left the bathroom, I went back to the room again for reasons I still don't understand. There was nothing there to see and there was nothing to say, but I couldn't fight a spirit that seemed to insist that I feel, yeah that's it, I had to feel that room. It was the room where Nana and mommy's life began and Mama Lou's life ended and I could visit her anytime I wanted. I felt a strange peace and a peculiar love in the room that I have never felt anywhere else. A child's imagination is strong indeed, but it is true that I have never entered a room since that time with such a strange brew of anxiety and welcome.

There was a lot of history in the old house and I had no choice but to hear almost all of it. I was about ten or eleven years old and everyone in my family was old. The women all wore orthopedic shoes and had salt and pepper hair covered with church sister hats. Mothball aroma mixed with perfume stuck to their coats. They always talked about something that happened fifty years before my birth. They enjoyed what I didn't understand. The after church dinner was always good, but everything seemed to come to a fuzzy halt, especially my childhood and the clock. Sagging skin and gaunt chins were before me, showing off aging dentures. I was always so awed by how teeth could move independently of the rest of the human face. Their dingy grins were full of praise; how pretty my dress was and how much I looked like my daddy as if I didn't know that. I knew I had to be seen and not heard in the old Gwynedd, Pennsylvania, house, leaving me with no one to talk to or play with. I have no siblings. In the summer, I went out onto the wraparound porch that overlooked lots of empty space—beautiful fields and a strange but comforting quiet; chipmunks and rabbits going about their day. I didn't know it was the land my great grandparents owned. I didn't know they had been slaves and earned their estate through unconscionable struggle. I didn't realize what that meant.

Back in the quiet fields of what used to be a fertile garden that fed my mother from birth, I saw an old rusted-out meat hook in the field and a small shack with some chipped green paint and a quarter moon carved on the door. Peeking inside, I looked down on what seemed to be a wooden bench with two large holes. The shack looked like a haunted house, and I didn't see how anyone would live in it, filled as it was with spider webs and bugs. Sometimes I played with the black and brown mutt, Pretty Girl, wondering how Cousin Verlie came up with the name. Pretty Girl was more than happy to drag me up and down Swedesford Road. Knowing the field better than I did, she took *me* for a walk.

     Cousin Joe and Verlie lived in the old house after my great grandmother's death in 1942 until Verlie died in 1980. Cousin Joe's mother was my grandmother's sister, Mary who died in May 1907 after giving birth to her hunchback son Joseph, so no one at the table knew much about her. Nana wasn't born until October of the same year. Luella, my great-grandmother, took care of her grandson Joe. He and Nana were more like brother and sister than aunt and nephew. Cousin Joe was a short and stumpy dark brown skinned man who loved his pipe and baseball. One of his shoes had a thick heel to accommodate his uneven legs. In spite of his handicap, he worked every day until he got too old. Cousin Joe's wife, Verlie Free was from Greensboro, North Carolina. Her ancestors dropped their slave name after emancipation. Cousin Verlie's chunky frame stood about five feet, three inches with coca brown skin. Her soft, silver hair beautifully crowned her kindly face. She usually had something nice for me; a puzzle or comic book to help me get through the grueling evening. Verlie had an awkward walk because her limbs bowed outward from having rickets as a child. She ran away from home to come north in the 1920s.

Sundays included visiting every shut-in all over Ambler and Penllyn. By the time my parents and I arrived at the old house, the church crew was already there and the table was loaded down with food. The food always smelled so good and the prayer always lasted too long. Cousin Verlie hobbled in the dining room carrying a big bowl of creamed corn "Alright now, time to eat." Cousin Joe was right behind her carrying the bird of the week. It could have been, a duck, goose, or turkey. A couple of times pheasant was under that cover. Everyone took their place at the table and bowed their heads. Cousin Joe led us in prayer.

"Let us pray......Lawd we thank you for bringing us here together...."

I was wondering to myself just how long this evening would be. I thought I got a whiff of turnips. I hate turnips. I hope mom doesn't make me eat them again. Maybe I'll get a chance to look at the Ed Sullivan show if Cousin Joe will let me. I always liked that show.

"Bless the hands that prepared the food for the nourishment of our bodies...."

Boots came crawling under the table snuggling around my feet. I felt the vibration from his purring. My stomach gurgled as the aroma of

the fresh baked bird teased my nose and steam
floating on top of the potatoes seemed to only
come my way. I was so hungry. I peeked to the
right where mom was sitting deep in prayer. When
Cousin Verlie greeted me earlier she said she had a
surprise for me. I wonder what it is.

"We thank ya Lawd for your grace...."
I guess we'll eat sooner or later. Old folks can sure
sit still for a long time. I peeked on the other side
and there was my dad. His head was in his lap too.
I should have brought my coloring book with me.

"In the name of the Father, the son and the Holy
Ghost.. Amen..."

Plates and bowls floated up and down the
table. I was able to pass those turnips without mom
noticing I didn't take any. Pretty Girl had her head
near my lap on the lookout for any unforeseen
accidents. I zoned out into myself for a while. I
gazed around the room when I could, looking at
nothing in particular but noticing details that
escaped grown people. Cracks had drawings
throughout the chalk white walls right up to the
toggle switch. The mirror above the ancient buffet
was hazy and peppered with black dots. I don't
think anything in the house was made in the 1900s.
I grabbed a biscuit while Missus Byrd was talking
and slipped my giblets to Pretty Girl. With a clean
plate in front of me, mom gave me permission to
leave the table with a nod of her head. After dinner,
I helped to clear the table and found my cozy spot,

which was wherever Boots and Pretty Girl were. They fought sometimes, but for the most part got along well as people and didn't seem to mind the extra company. I snuggled in' hoping not to be noticed; with nothing left to do, I listened. The old men always ended up in the living room after dinner and, with the most delightful pipe tobacco permeating the air, conversed about the ball game or the highlights of the deacon meeting. The women stayed in the dining room. They sipped tea, offered me cake, and every once in awhile looked down toward the floor at me with a feeble smile to make sure I was okay. Those old folks were not educated, but they had a lot to say. There were treasures in their heads and they were gonna 'sot' you down and tell you all about it. Entire evenings were spent getting it straight and they took no lip if they thought someone was wrong. When they disagreed, a lot of preaching took place to make their point clear. Work was hard and they got it done with pride. I heard things and saw pictures that meant nothing to me until years later.

My maternal grandmother, Nana, was Homzell Williams and loved to be the center of attention telling everything she knew about everyone. Her husband, my step grandfather, was William Govan. Pop-pop was a loving, low keyed dark skinned man with a potato sac physique who was totally illiterate and almost blind from glaucoma. He was owned by Nana. She was the lightest and the youngest of her brothers and sisters so her imagined birthright made her a bit presumptuous at times. Her bouncy gait and strawberry hair was quite a spectacle, especially when she entered a room. She lived in Bridgeport Connecticut so when she came to town everything, at least in her mind, was supposed to stop and focus on her. Her pancake makeup made a clear line around her neck and her eye shadow sometimes turned her eyebrows blue. Her demands were as high as her pride and her reciprocation was low. Nana liked to upstage the ladies who wore no makeup or perfume. To Nana, they had no style.

I didn't know the church sisters very well. They traveled in herds catching every dinner in town. I only saw them in church and at the Sunday dinners when Nana was in town. Miss Ida was a rather short dark skinned woman with a warm personality. She kept company with Cousin Verlie. They met weekly for scrabble games and church projects and spent afternoons making plans for the missionaries, the deacons auxiliary and Sunday banquets. Missus Byrd was a big black woman with squirrel gray hair who walked with a cane and had a little short stumpy man for a husband with a bad temper. She was nice to me; the only one who ever took time to talk to me. I didn't like her husband. When he got mad, he would foam and bubble and walk. I loved to watch old folks get mad. It put the fear of God in me, but at the same time it pulled back the veil to their otherwise holy demeanor. He was so angry, he once got up from the table in the middle of dinner, frothed and foamed out the door and walked all the way to North Wales where they lived. He had to walk, he couldn't drive. Missus Byrd drove. Missus Byrd was the first one to park at the table, all three hundred pounds of her. She always ate the biscuits—all of them. Miss Gladys was a nice fluffy faced woman with thin pitch black hair and a thick moustache whose daughter was one of the first in the area to have a house built. That was something. Most people bought houses that were already built. They all belonged to the NAACP and the Harriet Beecher Stowe Club. Along with cousin Verlie, Nana and my mother Hazel, they sat around the table most of the evening talking about the old days. I was hearing my history.

Boots was purring at my feet; Pretty Girl was sniffing my face and licking my hand every once in a while. I was listening.

"I don't really remember who was the meanest, the white folks or my family. I simply walked out of the house one morning and never looked back." Verlie said shaking her head looking down at her cake.   "Down home was bad for me. I couldn't wait to leave. I don't have nice memories like you all."

It was the perfect opportunity for Nana. Her eyes rolled toward the top of her head while her red rag almost hit her chin. She was ready.

"Not up here with momma and pappy. Dem people down there crazy! Oh ma gawd! The way we had to cook and clean and tend to the pigs and chickens, ain't that right Hazel?"

"That's right momma." my momma said.

"Joe'll tell ya. We used to laugh and talk while getting food together. The white folks was good to us. We had so much, we sold food to them! And didn't momma set a table?! Hazel was little, but she still had to help in the garden and in the kitchen, ain't that right Hazel?" Nana barked.

"That's right momma."

"Gawd knows we ate until we couldn't move. We had the best corn and tomatoes and pears. The table was loaded down with good food. We had everything. There wasn't no time for dirt and mess either. Momma would kill us, pappy too, but we had fun running out in the field picking berries and making ice cream. Ain't that right Hazel?" Nana talked like she was the star of the show.

"Yes momma."

I guess Nana had to catch her breath. She always talked that way to people especially when she knew they had had less. Nana was a little harsh to me too. She had a bite in her voice that could cut legs,
heads—hearts. Cousin Verlie was never confrontational and slow to anger, but her glassy

eyes seemed to indicate she may have been somewhat embarrassed or ashamed about her background, like in some way she was less than Nana. After some of Nana's rants Cousin Verlie's response wouldn't be any more than a defeated "Well I guess you're right" or "I don't know, maybe so." When cousin Verlie had that peculiar scratch to her otherwise jovial voice, I kind of felt sorry for her.

Except for the delicious homemade butter cake and milk, my mouth was shut and my body was still. My Buster Brown patent leathers were wearing on my pinky toes and my behind was numb. I would have given anything for my bunny slippers. I didn't feel connected to anything or anyone in the room except my mom and dad. Boots and Pretty Girl tried to be my friends, but they preferred to take a nap. The church sisters were leaving. I hoped we'd be next. It was another long event getting them out the door and into the car. It took at least fifteen minutes to get out of the back door, start the car, and get down the rock and stone driveway while the rest of us waved good bye until our arms were nearly dislocated. Cousin Verlie, Nana, and mom gathered back into the dining room. Dad, Pop-pop, and Cousin Joe were quietly watching television and nodding off. I took a minute to wander into the hallway just off from the dining room where there were pictures of Luella and Shadrach.

Nana said they were from Westmoreland County Virginia. My great -grandmother, Nana's mother, was Luella Fulcher who was born sometime in the 1850s along the Rappahannock River and migrated to Gwynedd, Pennsylvania sometime in the 1880s. Luella was born a slave on a dirt floor on the Fulcher plantation. She knew of her brother, Fred and one sister, Liza. Later, Luella told Hazel, her granddaughter, that she had vague memories of an older brother William before he was sold off.

"I think he was the oldest." Nana said. She never heard any talk of her grandfather. Luella never knew her father. Luella didn't know her mother for very long before she was sold off too. She was too young to know what was going on, but old enough to feel the pain.

"Yes Lawd. I remember some of the things grandmom used to say."
My mother continued. *"Grandmom said old massa whip people who didn't obey! She used to sprinkle pepper all over the house—something about keeping evil away from the house."*

Luella never knew her age. Nana said they went by the last storm or the phase of the moon to remember when someone was born or when they died, but she had some memory of when slavery ended. The vivid memories and fears of her childhood were with her for life. Once in a while, it seemed she didn't deliberately speak on them as much as a fragmented memory would pop out before she could catch it.

Momma later told me anybody from that end of Virginia knows about "The Neck" Machodoc Virginia, and The Hague. The only memory Luella had of her mother was her name, Betty. Betty was born in Ghana. Luella had dark smooth skin, average nose, small mouth, deep set hazel eyes and high cheek bones. Nana and my mother Hazel said Luella remembered a little bit of the Civil War and Abraham Lincoln.

"I remember momma said once how hard it was coming up as a young girl. Everything was upset. Nobody knew which way to go or what was coming next. Momma listened to the old folks talking about what they oughta do. She'd say she never saw coloreds so upset in her life. They was all running ass over tin cups to go north. Some were scared to leave, but they didn't want to stay." Nana said.

"I wonder how old she was?" mommy asked.

"She never knew her birthday, she said she was a little girl when the war was over, but who knows what that means. Teenagers were considered little girls. I wasn't grown myself until I was about thirty-five."

"Did your mother ever say what she did?" Verlie wondered.

"You know she never said too much about

that. As far as I know she stayed underneath Miss Thompson until she was up and married pappy." Nana continued.

"Now who was this Miss Thompson again?" my mother wondered. It was the first time I saw Nana look confused.

"Let me see now. I think it started with William's boy. William was my uncle. He had a son and later I think William was sold off. The boy grew up and had a child with Miss Thompson. That was Ella Jane. I don't know if they were married. From what momma said I think Ella Jane and momma were around the same age. So what dat make dem?" Nana looked at mom.

Mommy said "Well, I guess that made them…"

"They cousins." Verlie butted in with a figuring face.

"Was Miss Thompson the mother or the grandmother?" Verlie scratched her head.

"Naaaa! Now just hold on here" Nana was looking in the ceiling for answers.

"Oh Homzell! You dunno. Them old folks couldn't get it straight they self."

Cake crumbs dropped from Cousin Verlie's mouth onto the table and her lap. Pretty Girl sat up with a hopeful cock of her head. Mom finally spoke.

"I think Ella Jane was grandmom's great niece if she was William's grandchild. Even

though Miss Thompson was way older than grand
mom, she was grand mom's niece because she was
William's son's wife."

"I don't know if they was married." Nana
spoke.

"What the son's name?" asked mom.

"I dunno." Nana said.

"Did she ever mention her father?" mom
asked. "Na. You know how momma was. She only
told you a little bit. If you asked too many question
you might a slap in the mouth for being frishe.
Remember how she was Hazel? 'You keep dat red
rag in ya mouth.'" Nana said with a chuckle.

Cousin Verlie had a peculiar habit of picking
crumbs one by one off the table while thinking and
talking at the same time. Her limbs made it all the
more awkward.

" Well who sunnever they was, I'm sure they
all had to keep it low if they wanted to leave and
come up here—scared to go in the night, scared to
go in the day. It musta been a time. After coming
north, what cha gonna do? It was hard just to find
days' work."
Momma jumped in.

"*I remember grandmom talking a little bit
about that. She used to say "All you had to do was
agree with everything them white folks say, then
just keep on doin what you was doin. They never
know the difference. She'd say I members the old
folks back then saved money, got a horse and*

*buggy and was getting outta town, they come
north. I did the same when I got Shad."*

That was what Luella called my great-
grandfather sometimes. Other times she called him
Brother. His picture was beside hers in the
hallway—he didn't look too bad. I sat near the
caste iron floor vent piddling with the grooves in
the hunter green carpet thinking and looking at my
mother. I thought about my great-grandmother
being little girl and not having her mom and dad. I
looked at mom and thought about how much she
meant to me; how much time and love she gave to
me. I looked at my mother again and tried to
imagine if she just disappeared—to never hear her
voice or feel those hugs—never to know if she was
dead or alive.

Momma Lou belonged to Zion Baptist
Church and was baptized in the Rappahannock
River as a teen. Smoking a corn cob pipe in her
rocker, Luella told my mother how afraid she was
of old massa beating her and that he took her
family away. She saw others beaten and did what it
took to keep herself free from pain. She was
mostly quiet and just did as she was told. She lied
about what she knew and sneaked to do what was
necessary for her survival. She slept on a corn
fodder bed. Her striped cloth casings, called
ticking, were feedbags stuffed with fodder, wheat
chaff or leaves. Luella moved on with her life, but
was haunted by a pain in her youth nobody

understood. A heavy silence sometimes fell as the ladies began to imagine what it must have been like for Luella. Nobody really knew.

I drifted into the hallway again and looked at her picture hanging on the wall and thinking who was she really? I looked at that picture throughout my childhood. When I was little, that dead woman on the wall scared me. It was nothing more than an old woman who needed to comb her hair. But momma, Nana and Cousin Verlie had her traits on the table.
Momma Lou had wit. She carried pain. She told the ugly honest truth—and she loved mommy. As I grew older, her face grew kinder and wiser.

I saw where mommy looked a lot like her. Mom has her complexion and slightly raised cheekbones. I saw tender, wistful eyes they shared but didn't know that's what it was at the time. Mom and Nana couldn't be more different, but yet they had the same tendencies. They're both strong, but mom is gentle. They both knew how to save a nickel, prepare a delicious meal and hang out the whitest sheets. Mom could make anything alright with love and care. She was viewed as intelligent and determined by those who cared—hardheaded by those who couldn't beat it out of her. Some of that had to belong to Momma Lou. Mommy spoke up.

I think she was lonely and angry a lot times. That could be what made her prayer so strong. I

remember going to church with her and she
seemed at times to be a different person.
Everything that was held up inside came gushing
out.

"Momma was strong. She wasn't gonna let
nothing get to her. After a while she didn't pay that
mess no rabbit-assed mind."

It looked like Nana was trying to protect
Luella but it soon fell apart.

"Momma did have her way that nobody
understood. You know she didn't trust anyone,
especially white folks."

"Well who did?" Verlie muttered.

"Yea but momma preached about it." Nana
protested.

"Who didn't?" Verlie answered.

"Grandmom was never one to cry, but at
times she was despondent." mom thought.

"Desponse? Gal what you talking about?" It
would take Nana to get it twisted.

What I mean momma is I think grandmom
had dark places in her soul and would go off to
herself to cope with it as best she could.

Mom knew what she was talking about. She
had the same hole as a child missing her mother.

Pops was gone and she too proud to turn to
anyone. I remember she was afraid for me to get to
tight with friends. She didn't mind me having them,
but not too close. 'Every time they fart you come
stinkin!' she'd say. She never trusted white folks

and warned me not to either. Some of the Italians were okay, but she was afraid for me getting all up wit'em... by and by they talking nigger. She turned Technicolor when she got mad at'em. She'd say 'They a lie and the truth ain't in 'em. They know they done wrong and still say it ain't so. Had the nerve to go to church, but wasn't no Gawd in em' wit all that mess in they heart. They cheat us out of our money and land, steal our babies and whoop us if we cry. Then dey wants you to trust em. That's when they really get ya cause you start talking about things they can use against ya later on.

Mom's impersonation of her grandmother made the old lady in the picture come to life for me. Their voices became angry, sad and hurt barking back and forth at each other trying to figure first one legend then another. I didn't altogether understand, but I became a little upset myself.

My mother remembered looking in her grandmother's eyes and seeing the despair. Even on happy occasions, she had a fog that cast a shadow on her fragile face.

Mom only got parts of her grandmothers' story. Many of the old folks in mom's day were slaves as children but few would talk about it. Momma Lou said some things, but didn't talk too much about her enslavement and what she endured in her life, she didn't want to and after a while she refused to talk about it at all.

They dug into Shadrach. He was born somewhere in Westmoreland County, Virginia, and grew up on the Williams plantation. He also knew only two brothers and two sisters —John, Sam, Ida, and Patsy. All five were slaves as children but not impoverished. Nana remembered what her father Shadrach told her many years ago: He said they were treated better than most slaves. His parents were sold, but the children stayed together and came north when they were older. My great Uncle Sam ended up marrying Nana's sister-in-law, Martha Johnson. Shadrach never knew anything else about his people, who they were or where they came from.

"He said he thought he saw his momma once at Gwynedd Station and she thought he was her son." Nana continued. "I never knew how it all went down and pappy would never admit to tears. He only had a vague memory of her. The woman said "That's my boy and I knows it". Nana just looked as if she was wondering if it really was her grandmother. Shadrach never saw that woman again.

There is so much there that will never be known. Nobody could read or write and little was recorded; births, deaths or marriages. Some records were kept in church ledgers, but they're long gone. Neither of my great -grandparents ever celebrated a birthday or anniversary. Celebrations

were stolen from them, just like their families.
None of us ever knew the story of how they met or
when they were married. There was no church
service, no ring, and no license. We do know they
filled the house with lots of children.

I daydreamed about how they possibly met.
I imagined they lived nearby and possibly met at
church. Maybe Luella, with her Ghana roots, was a
descendent of the Ashanti tribe. She was strong,
proud and determined. Maybe Shadrach was a hell
raising warrior. They talked at church socials about
their determination for a better life. She probably
gave him a hard time at first. I can see them now
under a tree, talking, fussing, kissing and laughing.
I bet she was lonely, but had high expectations and
wouldn't take up with any ole farmer that smiled at
her. She fell in love with Shadrach's fearless
strength and his faith in their Father. He fell in love
with her passion for order, her belief in hard work
and her disdain for waywardness.

They knew together they could find a way
out—work on land they owned. Their hard work
kept their faith for each other strong and new.
Their mission was their romance. They may have
already known enough about each other to make
them comfortable together or other members of the
congregation thought they were a good fit and
encouraged them to 'take up'.

During the ride home that night I was left
with more questions than answers. I was so glad

to get that old folks musk out of my nose and back to my world. But a part of me was haunted by the spirits I heard so much about. I looked out the car window into a country darkness I had never seen, while thinking about people I never knew, wondering how to make sense of what I heard.

Every Thanksgiving holiday, my parents and I went to visit Nana in Fairfield County Connecticut, a suburb of Bridgeport; sometimes Cousin Joe and Verlie came with us. Nana lived in a Cape Cod house in a section of town called Chopsy Hill. Momma gave me a fresh Dixie Peach press and curl. In my sleep I dressed myself in blue bell bottom slacks, a turtle neck sweater and Pro Keds sneakers. I had packed my granny nightgown, tooth brush, my knitting needles and a Charlie Brown book the night before. I hated going up there. I wanted to be home with my friends. I knew of the parties I'd be missing and have to later suffer the agony of being the only one not there. Sitting around the old fogies meant I had to keep that smile and docile demeanor. It meant I had to leave the room when it filled with grown folks talk. I was welcome for waiting hand and foot for those too comfortable to wait on themselves.

Nana was pouncing around the kitchen when we arrived. She had just put the cranberry into the refrigerator to set. She made it the same way her mother made it. She stewed fresh cranberries with butter, vanilla, and sugar. She never measured anything, she just knew how much to put in. I could still smell it when I walked in the door. The house was full of people, but they were no kin to us. They were Nana's friends and had some down in the country names; Vela, Elmeeda, Braizell and Hercules. They were all dressed up in polka dots and plaids.

The main floor of Nana's house had two bedrooms, one bath, a large kitchen and a living room in which nobody was allowed, especially me. Downstairs had another full size kitchen, powder room and a colonial sitting room. She had two more bedrooms with slanted ceilings and bath on the top floor. That's where I stayed. I put my overnight bag away and opened a chest at the foot of the bed that had some puzzles and books that belonged to the daughter of white lady my grandmother worked for. The radio on the old telephone table next to the bed could get only one station. I turned on the small lamp burning a ten watt bulb and sat on the bed. I was thinking what a good time my friends must be having. The linoleum floor felt even colder as a loneliness settled into my bones.

"Terri come on down! What's taking you so long?!" Mom couldn't have been happier. Everyone had their little taste, getting happier by the minute.

Nana's living room had white area carpet

and white sofa and chairs. It was filled with antiques that belonged to my great-grandmother, Momma Lou. Mommy took me in the forbidden zone to see and even touch the antiques. Momma Lou's Chippendale table went the length of her bay window partially covered by a hand made scarf with an oil lamp that had been converted to electric some time ago. Mom pointed out the feet of the table noting the hand carved detail.

You can usually tell who made the furniture by the design of the skirt of the table and the feet.

I saw Momma Lou's rocking chair. She coddled my mother in that chair—the chair that nurtured my mother's heart. It sat on top of springs that gave a it slight bounce as I rocked back and forth. Tall lamps with evening gown shades were sitting on Duncan Phyfe end tables that were a part of Momma Lou's living room in Gwynedd.

All of this belonged to your great-grandmother and one day it will all be yours. Nana walked in the room weakening my knees. Since mom was with me, I could only be scathed with her notorious dagger eyes, as we stood by the curio cabinet in the corner.

"Momma! I can't believe this is still here, grandmom's salt and pepper shakers!"

"Pappy gave them to momma when he went to Atlantic City." Nana was our tour guide now. The red salt and pepper shakers read Atlantic City, 1904.

"And look at this momma, how did you save this pitcher?"

It was a green pressed glass pitcher that they both said was Momma Lou's favorite. She used it for her fresh lemonade or brewed iced tea they drank at almost every summertime meal.

"Momma said Florence gave it to her." Nana was inspecting her precious space for any clue of a violation.

"Who's Florence?" I wondered.

"She was your great aunt." Nana relaxed a little. "I was younger than you when she died. Lord knows momma went through something. First she lost Mary and was left to take care of Joe, then a few years later she lost Florence."

"Did aunt Florence have any kids?" I never looked Nana in the eye.

"No she didn't. She had those female problems. People didn't know what to do about those things back then. I gotta get to my greens and check my cassle dish." Nana left to tend to the big dinner.

"What's a cassle mom?"

She means casserole, the macaroni and cheese and don't say that too loud, you know how she is.

"Mommy how many was it of them anyway?"

It was thirteen from what I know. Some of them died before I was born and your grandmother was a little girl when some others died. Nana is the baby of the family. Some of the older ones were already grown by the time she came along. They were all born down the road. Only the last four or five were born in Gwynedd, not the house you know, there was another house on route 202. Only momma was born on Swedesford Road.

Mary, Florence, George and Florence's' husband 1900

I wasn't missing my friends as much. My mother always eased my pains. Besides, I was getting hungry and dinner was ready. The turkey and greens were cooking in the oven downstairs and the macaroni and cheese and rolls were upstairs. Nana never did like the smell of collards and turnip greens. She didn't want the smell in her custom drapes and carpet. Loud smelling foods were always cooked downstairs where she could close the door. Dad carried the big bird upstairs and Cousin Joe was right behind him with the greens. Cousin Verlie brought up the rear with the sweet potatoes and green beans. On the second tour, I brought up the gravy and sweet peas. Mom was right behind me with the creamed onions and those rotten turnips. Cousin Verlie got the fresh made cole slaw from the down stairs refrigerator. Nana was in the upstairs kitchen getting the macaroni out and putting the rolls in and mom told me to go to the refrigerator and get the ice water and cranberry sauce. The table was set with cloth napkins and candles sitting in hurricane holders; the bread plates were to the left just above the fork, and the stemmed water glasses were to the right. The plates were blue and white Meissen porcelain with sterling flatware.

Nana was front and center as usual assigning seats. I didn't care where I sat as long as I was next to mom. Nana and Pop-pop sat at the head and foot of the table.

"Alright every body. Terri turn that T.V. off. Govan, bless the table please."

Oh Lord, here we go.

After the blessing either my dad or pop-pop carved the turkey. Nana proudly wore her holiday apron, got the rolls out of the oven and prided herself to serve each one of us left hand service. She started near the head of the table with potatoes serving everyone from their left where they took a generous helping. On the second tour, she served each vegetable. She served the rolls last. She must have walked around that table five or six times serving everyone before she took her seat. Nobody served themselves except for seconds.

She required healthy praise for a job well done. If we forgot, she reminded us. "Everybody Happy?" She proudly bellowed at the end of her service. That was our clue to spend the rest of the evening telling her what a wonderful cook she was, how beautiful the table was—how beautiful *she* was.

Sweet potato pie and butter cake were for dessert with either chocolate or vanilla ice cream. Both were home made and totally cured my angst. I already knew my job was to clear the table. I was glad to get away from the noise. The dinner dishes stayed upstairs and cookware was washed downstairs. I went to the downstairs kitchen and took a good look at the mess. It was a large square

kitchen with long counters and deep cabinets.
Nana must have used every pot and pan she had. I
pulled up my sleeves and turned on the radio. I
found the Lux behind the apple and grapes curtains
on the sill and filled the sink with water while the
radio warmed up. It was a tall floor model radio
from the 1930s that Uncle Dawson bought and had
a pull-out drawer that was a record player. It only
played 78s. The men folks were coming
downstairs into the sitting room on the other side
of the steps. Cousin Joe, dad and pop-pop were
watching television, sitting and rocking and it
wasn't long before somebody was snoring. I was
about two hours washing dishes, wiping down the
bronze stove and sweeping the red and white
checker floor. I wasn't sure where everything
belonged, so I dried the pots and pans and placed
them on the metal pencil stripe table. It had
wooden legs and a flatware drawer on one side. I
wondered just how far back that table went. There
wasn't anything in that house that didn't have a
story behind it. I stood at the bottom of the stairs
and looked to the right at the now clean kitchen
and then to the left at the snoring trio and headed
upstairs. Nana and momma had taken care of
everything there and Nana's guests had just left. I
ducked upstairs to jump into my flannel granny
gown and matching robe and slippers. I wasn't
back downstairs one second.

"Go in that icebox and get some ice. Ain't

she something. That's my gal! Looking just like her daddy".
I think that scotch had touched Nana. Cousin Verlie and momma were hovered around that Haig and Haig pinch bottle scotch.

"Thank you Nana. I cleaned up everything down stairs, but I wasn't sure where to put some things." I took a seat next to mom.

"Oh dat's alright darlin! I'll tic care tomorrow. Come here and give me some sugar." Nana seemed to be so proud of me. It surprised me because I never said or did much of anything in her presence.

"Momma, I put Terri in private school. She's in fifth grade. She just got an A on her composition and she's still taking piano lessons!"
Now why did she have to get into that? I thought.

"Ain't that something? Lawd knows momma sure woulda been proud, wouldn't she? Sure wasn't no such thing as schoolin for us." Nana reflected. I saw her eyes for the first time. They were just like momma and momma Lou's— sad eyes trying to be happy.

"I had some schooling but it wasn't much. Ain't nobody had no time for school. We had to work." Nana remembered.
"What school did you go to momma?" my mother asked.

"I went to Spring House School, just like you, only I didn't go all the way. I don't think

Mary and Florence went at all; George, Lushy, none of 'em. It was only Alberta, Ella and me. The boys had to work. They knew how to count dat money! We needed good sense more than schooling. Hazel, you remember how momma was with somebody who was simpleminded? She'd say my gawd, you ain't sense enough to carry guts to a bear—looking like something sent for and couldn't make it!!"

Nana couldn't talk for laughing. Cousin Verlie was laughing, choking and coughing at the same time. The men folks were coming up from the basement to get ready for bed. Lights were turned off one by one and the house grew quiet. It was just us at the kitchen table. A brass chain lamp overhead kept us from being in the dark.

Momma you need to be quiet, you just like her! My mother snapped.

"Excuse me, Nana tell me more about my aunt Mary. What Happened to her?" I never heard much about her.

"She died before I was born. She was born down in Westmoleland. She was a little girl when momma and pappy came north. She married Joe Queenan. They lived in Asbury Park and she had a boy, that's your Cousin Joe. When Joe saw that his son wasn't right, I don't think he could do right and he just up and left."

"Shh. Joe'll hear ya!" Cousin Verlie warned. "You know he don't want to hear that talk."

Nana dropped a decibel.

"Mary was sick from having him, it tore her up so. After Joe left her, she had to fend for herself and the baby. She died in May, 1907 and little Joe was found with a dirty diaper and a bottle of sour milk by somebody up there. Momma and pappy got a wire to go up there. Mary was brought back here to bury." Nana paused to wet her throat. "Ain't never seen dat ole Joe since."

I remember Grandmom talking about it a little. She said that's why he went by the name of Williams and not Queenan. Florence married a man named White. She had two or three miscarriages. That's why she died. Never knew much about that man. After Florence died, he just went away.

Mommy looked at me as if to wonder what kind of heartache I had in store for her. It never crossed my mind to get into such a mess with the wrath of these old ladies that would be sure to come.

The next morning, I awoke to waffles, sage and fresh percolated coffee tickling my nose. I heard the old folks in the kitchen murmuring above the pop and crackle of sausage and clamoring of pots and pans. Nana rose early to spread a breakfast just as lavish as the dinner. She made her pancake batter from scratch and bought sage sausage from the Farmer's Market. She put clump butter in warmed maple syrup and had a beautiful dish of strawberry and pear preserves she canned herself. Fluffy scrambled eggs and hominy grits made my stomach pang for all of it. After breakfast we had to get back to Philly. Nana packed us up with her peaches, pears, corn, tomatoes and string beans in Ball glass jars. It took a good hour to pack the trunk with Nana's culinary loveliness. After another hour or so of good-byes, we left for home.

Luella Fulcher Williams, 1880s

My parents took me to many different places to eat on Sunday. I fell asleep at every church service at 59th Street Baptist Church. They dragged me from my hard bottom pew to the wide sofa seat of our 1961 Chrysler Windsor to dine at the Trott Inn on Haverford Avenue in West Philadelphia. During the early sixties, it was a well known black owned restaurant with soft blue décor, wall to wall carpet and candles burning dimly next to a basket of hot biscuits. Other times, we ate at the Marriott on City Avenue in the Fairfield Room or Stouffers in King of Prussia. On occasion we took a day trip down the White Horse Pike to Zaberers or to Atlantic City to Captain Starn's. About one Sunday a month after church, we had dinner with my mother's family in Gwynedd where I heard first one story then another of the woman who was in that picture hanging on the hallway wall. I gazed at that picture all day. I could not conceive of such a time so long ago.

With the help of Quakers, Shadrach left his pregnant wife in Virginia and headed for Pennsylvania. He got word from one of his brothers to come north to Gwynedd, Pennsylvania. He traveled back and forth from Virginia to Pennsylvania looking for work. Sometimes he went by horse and buggy, other times he hopped on the box car. Gone for months at a time, he worked in the field, the flour mill, in a foundry which was a small factory where metal castings were made located somewhere in North Wales and he shoed horses at Ole Ye Smith Shop in Gwynedd, Pa.

Nana and momma shared stories about what they remembered of how this house came to be theirs. It took a couple of years for Shadrach to save enough money and finally move north for good. Meanwhile Luella, alone with the children, kept house in a log cabin shack with a dirt floor in Tucker Hill, Virginia. He returned to Virginia one last time and got his wife and family and everyone headed up north for their new life. There was talk of a Doctor Bigalow who helped Shadrach get a job at the flour mill on Swedesford Road near the intersection of Rt. 202 and a small clap board shack for his growing family and land to farm. Within a few years Shadrach owned the property. He was trying to avoid the trap of sharecropping and wanted his own land. He didn't want to be caught in the endless trap of poverty and hopelessness. Soon after arriving, Luella gave birth to their son Clarence in 1885. He was the first child born in Pennsylvania.

"That's what everybody wanted. They wanted land to take care of their family. But they could never get the white man out of their way and to just leave them alone." Cousin Verlie's voice was just a little salty.

"Well they wasn't all like that up here cause

Doctor Bigalow was white and he was good to
pappy."

Here Nana goes again. "I ain't never heard
of no lynching and carrying on up here. We had the
Quakers and dem to help the cullards."

"Maybe, but they did stuff up here too, just
cause you didn't hear it don't mean it didn't
happen." Cousin Verlie shot back. That's right
cousin Verlie stand up on it.

"Ya'll didn't have Jim Crow, but you still
knew your place. You didn't walk in the front door
at the William Penn Inn."
Hot dog! It's getting good now!

Shadrach Williams,on Swedesford Road about 1910

My maternal grandmother Homzell Williams, 1914

Luella and Shadrach finally saved enough money and moved from their little shack on Rte. 202 to their home on Swedesford Road also in Gwynedd. Built in 1900, the house was new. Their last child, my grandmother, was born was in that house in the middle bedroom on October 13, 1907. Years later, in 1925, my mother was also born in the same house and the same room.

The old house had five small bedrooms, a living room and dining room, shed and eat-in kitchen and an attic with a small round window. A large apple tree and wraparound porch where my mother and her cousins slept sometimes on hot nights completed the front.

The shed kitchen, where the ice box sat, had two large windows and a door that led to the farm and a side door that led to the well. The window ledges were water tables where two clean aluminum buckets were filled with water and had a dipper. These buckets were filled the night before so there was water in the morning to wash-up in a basin. One step up led from the shed to the main kitchen. In mom's day, there was a linoleum floor kitchen and butter yellow walls with hunter green shades and a naked light bulb swinging from a chain, a wood burning stove, table and chairs and a corner curio cabinet.

Momma showed me where the artesian well used to be out the side back door. It was a pipe that was drilled deep into the earth until it hit a vein. A pump brought the water up and on the hottest July day the water was crystal clear and ice cold. It was the sweetest and purest water one could ever drink. Other people had dug wells, which wasn't as deep as a drilled one. Every time it rained there was plenty of water, but it was dirty and shared with snakes and rats and everything else, including underground seepage from the nearby outhouse. The Board of Health later closed them.

The coal bin and furnace were in the cellar. Electric was first installed in the 1920s and the bill was about a dollar fifty a month. Before you laugh don't forget the back breaking sunup to sundown work only meant about two dollars a week. Now try to laugh.

Their live stock included about five or six pigs and at times three hundred chickens and a cow named Black Betty. Pear, apple, birch, maple, hickory and walnut trees surrounded the grounds and berries grew every which a way; blackberries, strawberries, blueberries, jewberries and huckleberries.

Cats kept mice and weasels out of the chicken coop. Sometimes snakes came to the coop and sucked the eggs dry leaving two little holes on the side.

I went to gather eggs and all I saw were shells. When the cats had kittens, balls of fur ran rampant. I loved to play with them when I could, but after a while there were just too many. Uncle

Dawson gathered the kittens in a burlap bag and drowned them in the nearest pond. If they were allowed to live they would get sick, malnourished and diseased. Forget the vet. People didn't take themselves to the doctor much less the cats.

Next to the woodpile was the outhouse with the quarter moon on the hunter green door. Inside was a wooden bench with two carved holes. Newspaper was kept nearby. Many trips were made to the outhouse during the day and use of the slop bucket at night. Winter, spring, summer and fall— that's where everyone did their business. Mom tried to open the cob-webbed door of the dilapidated shack. I took a peek inside and it scared me to death. It was dark and buggy with a wood plank floor that had mostly rotted away. I couldn't believe it. People had to sit their behind on a wooden bench to do their business, sometimes two at a time— a luxury. Some people only had one hole.

We used the slop jars at night because it was a long and dark walk out here. Some people used a lantern but anything may be waiting for you like raccoons, possums and especially skunks. If you scare one of them it's all over. If somebody got sprayed by skunk, grandmom buried their clothes to get the smell out.

Talk about having a pot to piss in. Momma had a slop bucket, called chamber pot that was a toilet in the house. The fancy ones for the middle class came as a set: A large pitcher for water, a basin for daily wash ups, and a chamber pot. The chamber pot looked something like a large planter. I saw the big blue and white one on the floor in the dining room providing a home for a large plant. Affluent whites had a commode, like ones now in the hospital. It had a large pot with a comfortable seat. Poor folks had the slop bucket. It was just an old bucket with a lid and no toilet seat or any other comfort. Everyone had them. I tried to imagine having to clean up after white folks who disrespected me in sometimes the most dehumanizing manner; suck it up and humbly make their food, wash their clothes, pump their water, take care of the children, fight off their husband, and then to make matters worse, empty their stinking slops into the outhouse while they were comforted by their imagined superiority. Imagine coping with that, having to cope with that for one's own survival.

Some of the surrounding roads are Cowpath Road, now named Meeting House Road, Lantern Lane, Grasshopper Road and Gypsy Hill Road. Folklore says there were gypsy's through that stretch of road, thus the name. Mom said Momma Lou didn't like them.

She said they were conjures. Anybody who fooled with them ended up broke. They always wanted to tell other peoples' fortunes. I never known any of them to have a job. They wouldn't

*work in a pie shop eating every other pie. But they
stayed to themselves, never really bothered people.
Gypsy Hill Road was where they were. It was
almost like a camp. All through the area was
supposedly notorious for night doctors; medical
students who would lie in wait for a fresh body for
research. So if someone was walking the road
alone at night and wasn't ever seen again, it was
said the night doctors got 'em. Grandmom warned
me about walking those black roads by myself.*

Powerful locomotives, a product of the
industrial age, brought people to either Ambler or
Penllyn Station to walk a primitive journey in
darkness broken only by a kindle for guidance.
Silhouettes of giant trees arched the black sky.
Faint crackles of twigs and leaves beneath the feet
of scurrying night critters were the only sounds. It
must have been a lonely road to travel—a long
walk to refuge, especially for some who had no
light. A typical country night on a new moon
meant all that could be seen was a lantern floating
down the road as if it was on its own power. That
back road was Lantern Lane. One night mom took
me down that road coming home from Gwynedd.
The rear mirrors were pitch black. Not even a
lonesome house in the distance. Mommy stopped
the car for a second and turned off the head lights.
I thought I left this world.

*Try walking home in this! Creepy quiet, you
could hear a mouse piss on cotton. This is what it*

was like up home. Looking out the window didn't mean anything.

The country was definitely not for me. I heard the lonely train whistle in the distance and nothing else. I imagined a light about as powerful as a candle slowly floating toward me and begged momma to take me home.

Luella's children, my great aunts and uncles, grew up to be chauffeurs, butlers, maids and chefs. Some started out at the William Penn Inn Hotel in the 1910s and 1920s. This prestigious establishment dating back to the early1700s is a restaurant, bed and breakfast. No coloreds were allowed through the front door. Uncle Clarence had to go through the back door to the kitchen and cooked some of the best food in town to elegantly nourish the very people who oppressed them. Uncle George had his own business. Like everyone else he had a farm to feed his family. He bought an old toll gate house for the Penllyn-Bluebell Turnpike and in years to come turned it into a beautiful home.

We didn't have thrift shops. When the old folks died, or people moved, they put stuff out. Uncle George collected all of it and got nice furniture and a beautiful piano. He helped other people furnish their houses too. Some of that stuff would be worth a fortune today. He was up at the crack of dawn until late at night, running his farm and doing his junk route. People used to call him

'Sleeping Jesus' because he was behind the wheel of his truck fighting to stay awake and praying to Jesus to help him through it.

We went to Penllyn on occasion to visit people momma told me were my third cousins. Uncle George's house put me in mind of Vicky Lawrence and Carol Burnett's *Mama's Family*. It was modest and clean in 1940s décor. Uncle George never really knew who I was. He was the first senile person I ever saw. He was happy to see everybody, no matter who they were. My cousins are his grandchildren. They took me out to the sprawling back yard for a game of horseshoes and volleyball. In the back of the yard was a garden filled with red shiny tomatoes and deep, maple leaf green cucumbers. A couple of corn stalks were right next to the garage where Uncle George's 1930 something truck had been parked for about sixty years. Momma told me about that truck. It was with that truck he was able to buy the house. He cleaned up junk and collected garbage from restaurants and over-the-counter stores called the American Store to feed his pigs and keep the kitchen table going. The American Store was the general store stocking everything from dry goods to fruits and vegetables. There were only a few: Ambler, North Wales and another at Broad and Erie in Philadelphia. In the late fifties it became Atlantic and Pacific supermarket known as the A&P. Over the years more stores and restaurants came along. Uncle George, longing to read and write, continued collecting garbage and sold it to other farmers. After World War II and through the fifties supermarkets came in and his no named garbage business grew bigger through which he bought half of Penllyn, sent all seven children to college and gave them land to build their home for wedding gifts.

My parents and I had an occasional to visit for whatever reason. Uncle George's daughters, Nanny Ella and Astoria prepared a sprawling dinner for everyone. Nothing came from the supermarket. All vegetables were from their garden and meats were from the butcher or the slaughterhouse in Hatfield. They didn't trust Styrofoam and plastic. They were used hand picking their food. Only a squeeze from experienced hands could determine what was fit for stewing or canning. After Thanksgiving, Trewellyn Avenue was lined with pigs hanging from trees, a sight I never became fully accustomed to, nor connected with my joyful visits to smoked ham dinners.

After dinner momma and her cousins Nanny Ella, Astoria and cousin Herb reminisced about their childhood. Nana wasn't in town, so other people now had a chance to talk. My cousins and I began to listen when we were too tired to play anymore. My cousin Lolly was country sweet and kind, butter yellow skin and thick brown hair. Her smile made me love her instantly. Her older sister Kay was about the same, but more laid back. Their company was such a relief. I didn't mind the family visits as much as when I was in Gwynedd. Lolly and I could share a head nod or giggle while munching on home made ice cream and warm apple pie. The dining room table was surrounded with mommy and her cousins talking about when they were kids. After Saturday morning chores, they trekked to the stores in Ambler. Everything was over-the-counter. They bought flour, rice, meal and salt. Sugar and salt came in little cloth bags. Rice and other grains, sometimes had mites, were stored in big barrels with no lids and maybe a cat snoozing on top. The storekeeper needed the cats to keep the mice away and cat hairs were in the rice and flour. The storekeeper just shook off the hair and passed it to the customer. Raw milk, notorious for Diphtheria, was dipped from unrefrigerated vessels into bottles. People got sick, and some died, particularly children. Everyone was vulnerable to disease. The Board of Health came through and shut all those stores down before the war. The benefits of pasteurization were well known, but it was only used in ale and was not yet the law. Food could be dirty, but people, both black and white, didn't know anything about bacteria. They hardly had soap and water.

I often asked mom about her life as a child. I wanted to know if she played the same games and liked the same things as I did. Her world was so different from mine. I ate cereal in my pajamas and watched Saturday morning cartoons. In the winter, a touch of the thermostat kept the house warm. It wasn't true for her. Not one convenience existed for her. For the most part, it didn't exist at all. She didn't hesitate to explain to me how it was. She didn't leave out anything.

Chopping trees created kindling which is a thin poor grade of wood, but good for starting fires. They started the fire with the kindling then put the logs in the Franklin stove and after it caught it started to burn pretty well. In the winter they put coal called anthracite, on top of that. That was a good hard fire for heating and cooking. Coal was ordered by the ton, the old folks called it 'turn'. Anthracite burns long, hard and heavy, favored for the winter. Peat coal; it's a gravel like mineral, was used for summertime or when a softer heat was desired. I had to be up first thing to get the embers from the coal and sprinkle them outside to melt the ice and snow in the winter.

Just about everyone ordered three tons of coal to get through the winter. It was cheaper to buy it in August than in November. They even named a town after the amount of coal everyone bought. Three Tons is just above Jarrettown. Once the fire got going, the top of the stove glowed bright red, and none of the children ever got burned and the house never caught fire. That's

*back when children did what they were told. No
time out. Touch it and die, and they meant it.
People had no education but they could ill afford
to be stupid. It's called cruel now, but when
children didn't obey, they got their behind torn up.
Mom, dad, aunt, uncle, grandmom, it didn't matter.
We didn't have problems with self esteem, we
didn't know those words back then. We just did it
and there were no problems from any child.*

*We had a wood lifter to lift the top plate on
the stove and fed the fire with trash. The draft was
turned up for a high fire and turned down to keep
it low. An asbestos panel lined the wall behind the
stove. We had a basket to empty the ashes and a
coal scuttle along side the stove. The coal man
dumped the coal into the basement through a
chute. We had a furnace to heat the downstairs and
a pot belly stove for upstairs.*

*On occasion, snakes and rats were buried in
the coal, sometimes dead, sometimes alive.
Grandmom got a big stick from the tree and poked
the pile to inspect it. Just to make sure, a couple of
cats were put in the basement in case a snack
popped up. Once in a while Grandmom caught a
snake and threw it in the furnace along with the
coal. Anyway, I think coal was about ten dollars a
ton, so that's thirty dollars—more than a month's
pay. That's when folks had house rent parties, took
in extra laundry or worked late 'doing dinners'.*

I heard Nana talking about doing dinners for

her *madam*. Doing dinners meant that in addition to doing the regular house maid work, just like any other nine to five, house maids stayed most of the evening to serve lavish late night dinners for their employers. It was extra pay and usually mighty tasty and expensive leftovers to bring home. Nana prided herself in having the stamina of being an endless servant to white folks.

Momma had to stay in front of the red hot stove to keep warm. Everyone did. Hot tea or cocoa added to their warmth. Momma read bible passages to her grandmother as she often did to me. In the absence of phones and televisions, they made their own fun. Their slower pace of life provided songs, spoon bread and mended socks. Kerosene or 'earl' lamps were still used even after they had electric. Sitting in front of the fire kept their front warm and their back cold.

We had some terrible storms. I woke up looking at nothing but white— not even a break in the snow. Snowstorms shut down everything. It may be a few days before anybody could get out. Gwynedd didn't have snow plows. There wasn't anywhere to go anyway. Uncle Dossy shoveled a path so Dorothy and me could feed the chickens and pigs and get some firewood. We sat in front of the fire and every once in a while a spark jumped out. Sometimes it missed and other times it hit us dead on leaving burns we called fire blossoms. I played the piano to pass the time. We had a player piano with peddles and rollers. That's how I learned chords. When I got a song in my head, I figured it out. I loved to sing around the house. When uncle Dossy came in I had to stop. "Cut all dat noise out gal. Stop dummin on that piana!"

What did Momma Lou think about your singing and playing? I asked mom.

She never said one way or the other. It didn't seem to bother her or impress her, but she never encouraged it. You gotta remember, these were hard times and the only thing anybody worried about was where the next penny was coming from. Music to them was a waste of time except in church.

Cousin Verlie, Aunt Ella and her daughter Mary, mom and me all piled up in the car and went north on Route 309 one hot day. Montgomery Mall didn't exist. The 309 cinema featured drive-in movies. We went to a roadside fruit and vegetable store that displayed the freshest produce. Sometimes there were more bees than people. A guy in the back was hacking up watermelon for people who only wanted to buy half. Mama and them bought up boxes of everything and hauled it back to the old house. I helped to unload, snacking on peaches and grapes all the while. It was just like the old days mom often talked about. The kitchen was full of women washing veggies, shucking and boiling corn, tossing salad and making lemonade. Summer smells permeated the house as the late afternoon sun splashed through the window. The delightful scene created jubilance in everyone including the cats and dogs. I played with them and even managed to sneak a hunk of tuna for Boots. After a light but filling summer meal the ladies convened on the front porch when the bugs weren't too bad. Sometime Aunt Ella's other daughter, Tina, came by with her three daughters who were about my age. Cousin Joe went into the backyard after dinner to burn the trash. We were already having a nice time and an open fire added to it. As the sun disappeared behind the trees, we gathered up leaves and sticks, newspaper and anything else that could burn and brought out it back. We stood back while dad and Cousin Joe started the fire and watched it grow. Cousin Verlie told us to go out and get a stick while she hobbled into the kitchen toward the white metal cupboard and brought out an unopened bag of marshmallows. It was just like when mom was a little girl. My skin was prickly with heat while we were watching the consuming power of fire, roasting marshmallows and playing tag. We freely rolled in the field giggling for no reason and stuffing too many marshmallows in our mouths at once. "Not too close now!" Cousin Joe bellowed while forking dead shrubs into the fire. "Y'all take care, get back now!!"

After the lightning bugs got on our nerves and the old folks were talked out, everyone started to pack up for home. Tina and her girls left first. I went upstairs to visit the room. It was a wonderful way to end the day knowing Momma Lou was looking down on all of us. I sat there with that strange feeling I didn't care to share with my cousins. The spell was broken when mom hollered from the front to get a move on. "Gotta go Momma Lou! I'll be back to see you soon."

Wisdom and Faith

My great-grandmother, Luella knew the likes of people well. She was suspicious of peoples' motives and on guard. "There's a heap that sees, but a damn few that know," Luella always told my mother. "People live and tell lies all the time. Nobody knows where the nose goes when the doe's closed. People smile and lie while they're sneaking and deceiving." Luella's timeless doctrine ensured deliverance from wicked traps people were sure to set. Mom and I were enjoying a full moon on a sultry summer night.

Let me tell you about your great-grandmother. She could read that moon like a map. She could tell when a woman was about to give birth by that moon. If a quarter moon had the two points facing up, that meant we were in for a dry spell, if they faced down, that meant rain. She read people just as well. She never gave a damn what anyone did. She didn't bother too much with people outside of church and family and never wanted to be bothered. Tending to her own business kept her busy enough. She loved her grandchildren and gave all the love she had to them, but she was stern. When it was time to get work done she didn't take any back talk or disobedience of any kind. She kept order and it didn't require a lot of hollering and whipping. She may have knocked me out once. That was for me to get it. After that there wasn't any problem. I saw her making dough for bread, boiling clothes in the yard, and tending to the farm. Poor soul, she never sat down until long after dinner. She worked day and night and there was no way anyone was going to do to suit themselves when there was work to be done. Everyone had a job to do and they did it. There wasn't anything left to say. When I was about seven or eight years old, grandmom started me off gathering eggs from the coop, picking vegetables and washing them off and gathering straw to make a nest for the hens. She kept the house clean, got the cooking done, kept the farm in order and took in laundry to make money. She could not stand mindless, thoughtless and trifling people.

Mom had a little taste with her and so did I.

You know in some ways, you're just like her. Luella never did like people hanging around too much or too long. They wore on her patience.

"Mom, I just get tired of the same conversation from the same people all the time— rearranging my priorities—smiling and lying and telling me what to like."

And I'm telling you, you got it honest. She didn't have patience for a bunch of bullshit, and you just like her. Sitting and talking too much was trouble to grandmom, a breeding ground for contempt. She wondered how much was there to talk about with the same people. After a while they gonna get to lying and talking about folks. There's the trouble grandmom didn't like. She'd sit there

Wisdom and Faith

for a little while, but she got tired of it.

"Well what in the devil happened to Aunt Bert, Aunt Ella and Nana. They can take it home talking about stuff."

It was a social outlet for them, but they kept most of it away from grandmom.

"I guess it was the times momma. After all, most people didn't have radio or telephone and television wasn't out yet. People didn't have anything else to do."

Mom told me they lived a hard, but simple life that required nothing but common sense and a strong back. Entertainment was eating and talking. In spite of that, all of Luella's children grew up, barely able to read or write and bought land, houses and cars during The Depression.

Momma Lou wasn't easily swayed from her sensibilities nor influenced by the outside world. She had no faith in people and no concern for the politics of this country. Her trust was in the good Lord. Anyone approaching her with begging and borrowing games was abruptly dismissed.

"Never let anyone do but so much for you" Momma Lou preached. "Some people will think they own you and you'll never repay the debt and they'll never let you forget it. I was already owned once." Momma Lou didn't trust big grins. Wide smiles and shifty eyes with a mouth full of someone else's dirt was bad news. She concluded they were deceitful. "Dog bring a bone, carry a bone. You gotta watch people always in ya face talking bad about people. They tell everybody else's dirt but their own." Momma Lou stormed. "You never know the length of a snake until you stretch him out." was said by almost everyone.

You see, Grandmom was leery of people. They put her in mind of snakes. You remember that story momma told about the man and the snake?

"I think so."

"Well let me tell you again. An old man found a frozen snake in the woods and brought him home to thaw him out. The old man put him in front of the fire and gave him food and comfort. When the snake finally warmed up and came back to itself, it turned around and bit the man. The appalled man said 'How could you do that to me? I found you frozen in the woods gave you soup and a blanket and put you in front of the fire to warm up. Now you turn around and bite me. Why would you do such a thing?' The snake answered 'You knew I was a snake when you brought me in.'

That's people. They do shit like that. They come off very nice, with that notorious smile, play helpless or genuine until they think they have your trust. Then they'll bite you. That's why grandmom didn't like a grinned-toothed woman.

I knew Momma Lou for the first time. I was old enough feel her wisdom—the wisdom that knows it's times that change, not people.

You know how people just run all over top

of folks trying to have their way over and over again and it never comes out right? They start telling you first one thing, then another and the next thing you know, you're all balled up in a knot and wonder how you got there. Grandmom hated that pot stirring shit. She just say that's their little red wagon, they can push it— or they can pull it. She was tired of it all by then.

You know the average woman will run her mouth and the truth usually ain't enough. Before it's through, she's got to lie; tell-a-graph, tell-a-phone, tell-a-woman. It's all the same, ain't it? And they always come off as nice. Watch those smiling bitches—they deceitful.

I remember when I was a child I wouldn't dare say a word but they did some of the same things as everyone else. Before the funk left the chair, my great aunts were talking about the person who just left.

"But momma, what about Nana? She carried tales from Bridgeport Connecticut to Westmoreland County Virginia". I chuckled. Hard to believe were mother and daughter.

That ain't got nothing to do with it. I heard your grandmother tear people down for running their mouth, and then she'd turn around and talk about the same people who talked about other people.

Since girl to girl has been so unjust—I hardly know which one to trust—I've trusted many

Wisdom and Faith

to my sorrow—You trust today and I'll trust tomorrow.

"You always told me that women will stand at your back and see your face well bruised. They'll tell some of their business as bait, and then try to trick you into telling yours; come off as a friend and the next thing you know they're sniffing your man and spreading your name. They thrived on gossip and jealousy over just about anything— differences in complexion, weight, hair, clothes or intelligence. It could be anything that showed them what they're not."

"To grandmom women were bad luck anyway. One year, I'll never forget Aunt Nina was the first to enter the house on New Years Day. Grandmom had a fit. Don't you know that year just about all of her chickens died? The ones that didn't die didn't set. She had a terrible year. I don't think she ever forgave Aunt Nina for that."

I heard constant reprimands of a variety of absent perpetrators; black and white; men and women; young and old. Damned if you do, damned if you don't. If your skin is light, you must think you're cute, if it's dark you're ugly. Wear a nice dress, you think you're hi-fi, wear a cheap one and you're tacky. If you have a man he must be someone else's husband, if you have no man, there is something wrong with you. Have an ugly man then that's all you could get, have a handsome man and he's just using you. The only good men were their brothers and husbands. Men folks didn't catch a break either. They drank, gambled, and were whore mongrels, liars, or kicking women's ass.

"I remember you telling me when you were a little girl how Momma Lou, Uncle Dawson and Aunt Rosie talked about the time they had working for the white folks. They went through didn't they?"

Had to watch'em. Some were awful lowdown. They were forever trying to cheat coloreds out of what they owed them, then turn their ass up. I told you about that time when the boss man called Uncle Earl a nigger! He told Earl to clean up after the dog. Uncle Earl was the butler and chauffeur; he wasn't about to clean up some dog shit. One word led to another and the boss man called Earl out. Well sir! Uncle Earl picked up a milk bottle ready to come down on him. The Gardner came between'em; told Uncle Earl how hard it would be; hittin a white man. Uncle Earl walked out the house and got another job down the street! Aunt Rosie cussed out the white woman she worked for. She was talking shit about if it wasn't for her, Aunt Rosie would be starving. Aunt Rosie said to her as long as your husband got a job, I'll never be broke.

"Lord Momma, she got down with him?"

How would I know? You know what grandmom said about that nose when the doors closed! What I'm saying is that they were liberated before it was popular. They didn't take no shit from nobody, black or white.

"Aunt Bert didn't seem to be that way."

That's because she liked making that money. Aunt Bert worked around them. She didn't kiss their ass, but she didn't get too tight with them. You know Aunt Bert and Uncle Bill had a car for a long time. I don't think her madam ever knew. She didn't know when they got a television set either. You couldn't let 'em know too much cause they think you uppity. Colored voted up here, but the white folks told 'em who to vote for. I can't say they pulled the lever they were told, but coloreds had to let them believe they did. Uncle George and Aunt Bert were Republicans. They didn't change until Roosevelt ran for office.

"They were all ears with white folks when it came to money. That was the only time I ever heard anybody taking up what white folks said. Momma, you had to watch the old folks, the white folks, the men folks and all of the stuff they said and did, but you kept your spirit and managed to stay free. You never shut me down as a child. You hung on to your self. I never had to lie to you to keep the peace." I always admired how she easily touched people.

I know the damage shutting children down can do—the resentment it breeds. It does more to create sneaks and liars. People lock their kids up with what they think and then when something happens, they're shocked and devastated. If I didn't let you talk, I'll never know what you're thinking, I can't deal with something I don't know about. That's why we talked. Only then can I guide and direct. How else would I ever know you? That's the real old school—having some damn sense and a hell of a lot of imagination.

Wisdom and Faith

Bethlehem Baptist Church is located in Penllyn, Pennsylvania. Founded in1888, it was the spiritual and political foundation of the community. The Ku Klux Klan bombed our nice little church in February 18, 1964, but was rebuilt the next year and re-dedicated in October 1965. Black churches were being bombed all over. The year before, four little girls were killed at the 16th Street Baptist church in Birmingham, Alabama. Shadrach was a member of the deacon board in the early days of Bethlehem Baptist Church and Reverend Caesar Edwards was pastor. Penllyn is about five miles south of Gwynedd and was settled by the Dutch and Welsh.

Caesar Edwards was born a slave in Westmoreland County. He was older than Luella and Shadrach. Mom said she heard from grandmom that he found his way to Gwynedd. She wasn't sure if it was the Underground Railroad, but positive the Quakers helped. He didn't want to go to the city because he wanted land to farm. Later, he sent for his wife to be with him and from there the word spread throughout Westmoreland County to come north to Gwynedd. Shadrach's brother's, Sam and John came up and later so did Shadrach.

The small church had plank floors and no piano. It was headquarters for strength, solace and fun. The church began with a small group of people who met for prayer meeting at a private home in Spring House. As the population grew, they moved to a building on Old Penllyn Pike. The members put their money together to buy more land to build a larger church that was dedicated October 1905. Just about everyone from this generation down was married, christened and eulogized from that church. Reverend Quann is pastor now. Before the church pool, people were baptized near Wilson's dam in Ambler. Bethlehem church was the center of Penllyn population. The sister church, Zion Baptist, is on North Street in Ambler.

Getting ready for church started with the Saturday night bath. I took a lye soap bath in the tin tub in the kitchen. I greased down with petroleum jelly or goose grease. Aunt Rosie did my hair while grandmom got herself together. We were up first thing Sunday morning. Grandmom had the fire roaring for breakfast. Just the smell of the wood fire made me hungry. We had sage sausage and smoked ham from the smoke house, pancakes from scratch covered with molasses and butter— ice cold milk, fresh brewed tea and fluffy fresh eggs. She sifted flour sugar, baking powder and a pinch of salt together; then she added two eggs, a little oil and about a half cup milk and beat up a good batter. She poured the batter on that caste iron spider. Talkin bout something good!

I wore the only Sunday dress I had. Grandmom kept it clean and pressed. I didn't go to Penllyn for Sunday school; I went to Zion in Ambler. I went to Penllyn for church service.

"Why?" I wondered.

Transportation. There was no way to get from Gwynedd to Penllyn. I caught the Leigh Valley bus in front of the William Penn Inn to go to Ambler. After Sunday school I caught the train in Ambler to go to Penllyn and walked up the road.

"You had to go through all of that?" It was too round about.

It wasn't a choice, especially Sunday school. I started singing in school, but church was where I sang the most. I loved music ever since. I got that from my fathers' people, the Johnson's. The Williams' family couldn't hold a note in a coffee cup. I joined the junior choir when I was about eight or nine and looked forward to doing solos. It was the only day I had to see my cousins and friends. My Sunday school teacher, Missus Holden, opened up with a prayer and a song—Bring in the Sheaves or Blessed Assurance. Sometimes I was allowed to lead. Then we had to recite a passage from the Bible. Most recited psalms or their favorite passage from a verse. After Sunday school, we gathered at Brunson's store. That's where I saw the Home girls. We used to talk and joke around a little bit. It was the only time we could talk without getting in trouble. We used to kid around, but made sure the old folks were far away. We had fun singing dirty riddles we knew they wouldn't tolerate.

"What kind of riddles?" I thought about my schoolyard days.

Wisdom and Faith

Ham and eggs fried in snot, eighteen assholes tied in a knot!

"You're kidding!" Mom had me cracking up.

Not at all. We had a little hand clap or sometimes we skipped around each other.

Fat and funky from the country how much is your geese? Big and shitty from the city fifty cents apiece!

You're head is so nappy, who in the world was your pappy— you're bow legged, box ankled and slew footed too— the sins of the whole world musta fell on you! We had so much fun with that. Then I made my way to Penllyn church. Grandmom was already there.

"I know Momma Lou would've slapped you silly had she heard you say that."

"All them old folk would've. It didn't matter who heard. We kept that little dirt to ourselves. That's what made it fun. Anyway, after Sunday school I had to make my way to church in Penllyn."

"How did she get from Gwynedd to Penllyn?" I wondered.

Her son, Uncle George. You know he lived in Penllyn. He clackity clacked in that raggedy truck to pick up grandmom. After church grandmom and me went to his house for dinner. He had seven children, my first cousins. It was the after church social. Sometimes Grandmom cooked on Sunday's when she didn't go to church. When evening came,

Wisdom and Faith

Uncle George took grandmom and me back to Gwynedd. He had to crank up that truck to get it going. Clackity, clackity, clack. That truck was so noisy. You could hear it all the way to Penllyn Station.

Momma said Momma Lou was a hard praying woman. Known as Sister Ella to her church family, she got up that first Sunday and walked the floor with tears streaming down her face. When she got the ghost, she walked praising our Heavenly Father. Mom saw her grandmother in prayer; a mighty march down the aisle or on her knees in a holy moment of sanctity opening the desires of my mother's heart that was yearning to feel an ultimate love no mortal can provide.

My gawd chile it just gets in you. There is no way you could sit still with so much emotion in the chapel. When she started getting happy and clapping her hands, I was happy too. I tell ya, you'd do some funny things tryin to sit still. Mom told me crying sometimes herself.

It was the kind of prayer that kept us strong. It gave us the guts to face what we had to do. People don't have it now like we had it then. They go to church and take communion, but do they have Gawd in em? Struggle will give you power and nerve, but you need Gawd to put it on the right road otherwise you just get mad and gonna do wrong.

When I've come to the end of my journey and weary of life but the battle is won— carrying the staff and the cross of redemption— He'll understand and say well done —my good and faithful servant— come on home, just come on home—Pick up your cross and walk. People don't pray like that anymore. That's the worship I came up with. It was a beautiful thing. All of our troubles flowed like water— with every breath and fiber of our bodies, we were the embodiment of Jesus—we came unto Him as a little child to be cleansed and healed, mom testified. *Sister Edwards, Sister Martha Williams, Miss Nanny Lee, Mr. Ed Lee tore up Sunday morning. That was church— that was worship. I had the garden of prayer, the harvest of hope and a crop of strength.*

I felt like I had just had meeting myself. Something flowed through me. If those folks could cope with all they had going against them, no way in hell am I ever going to settle for something cheap without a fight.

Nana and her sisters had other ideas when they were in church. I used to love to sit behind them, especially at funerals. I pretended like I didn't hear a word. They had a name for everybody in the church standing lord and master over imperfections they happened to have themselves. They would cut their eyes, nod their heads and hunch each other signifying about other people cracking up laughing. Uncle Clarence mocked the minister. Nana and Aunt Bert raked over the choir while Aunt Ella took attendance of the congregation.

They didn't pass the plate in those days. People walked down the aisle to the alter to place their offering. People who wanted to show off their outfit always took the long way around the entire church before walking down the center aisle. Aunt Ella and momma picked apart everybody in the fashion show. Aunt Ella hunched momma.

"Homzell, look at dem shoes. And dat head, my gawd. It look like rats been pissin in it." Momma sittin up there laughing and hunching Aunt Bert.

"Did you see dat hat?" I don't think they heard anything the reverend said.

Wisdom and Faith

Aunt Bert and Aunt Nina around 1920

Me and my friend Emma saved makeup we bought at the dime store for church. We were too grown to sit up front. We sat in the back so we could do our little devilment. I was getting ready for the cellaret, a church basement party for teens after church. I never will forget it. The makeup was Park and Tilford. I had the compact and lipstick. I popped that compact puffing myself up and who do I catch in the mirror but Miss Martha sitting behind me. She shook her finger at me and I stuck my tongue out in the mirror. I thought I was smart. I got a supreme shakedown when I got home from church. I never did know how those old folks did it. Word got back to grandmom before I got home and nobody had a phone.

Emma and I had a little money from working for the white folks. We went up on Butler Avenue to the five and ten cent store and bought up nail polish and perfume. We had to sneak. If grandmom caught me with it, she'd have a fit. Gittin too omnish— smelling your funk! That stuff was only for fast women, not young ladies. She didn't like it at all.

We painted our toes as soon as we got out of the store. We were so full of ourselves. We walked up the avenue just as proud as a dog with a rose up his ass! Well sir, who do we run into but Reverend Holden! I guess he saw the devil in us cause the first place he looked was down at our feet. "Going down mighty low with that stuff!" Me and Emma took off.

After church, Nana's sisters and brothers with their spouses and children visited the family home. Under the apple tree was a long bench where the women folk sat and talked. The men sat back in the yard. A foot tub sat in the back filled to the brim with ice cold lemonade. It was kept cold by a twenty five cent block of ice as clear as glass and had a dipper for everyone to fill their glass.

Turning the corner onto Swedesford Road the smell was just too much. In the middle of the Great Depression, the table was set with roast chickens that were knocked in the head the day before; ham butt with a pot of string beans right out the garden. Summertime meant a lot of corn on the cob, peach and apple cobbler and big pans of macaroni and cheese. Cinnamon buns were made with brown sugar and real cinnamon from the stick. Children ran around filled with laughter while the men folk stood in the back of the yard with a brown paper bag, keeping it quiet. Children delivered a plate to the old folks who couldn't get out. The more family came, the better it was. Not one hungry belly in all of Penllyn and Gwynedd.

Sometimes we went to Ambler on Sundays after dinner to watch the trains come by. I tell ya, when that train blew in, it was something else. You could feel the wind all the way down South Ambler; it would suck you under if you got too close. Rich white folks rode Pullman. It was a big black locomotive; they called it the Black Diamond. I saw the men in the back pitching and poking coal. It was grand living on those trains with linen table clothes and flowers, waiters and butlers; they even had berths. Your grandfather, Eddie Johnson was a Pullman chef on that train. People spent Sunday afternoons at the station waiting for it to pull in. Several lines passed through Ambler—the B&O, Pennsylvania and the Chesapeake—but that Black Diamond beat it all.

When I was a child, we rarely visited Penllyn or Gwynedd over Christmas. Mom had friends to visit, parties to give and affairs to attend. I enjoyed my Christmas well enough without them and welcomed a time not having to go. I didn't find them to be particularly festive people. I enjoyed the children of my parents' friends much more. Momma always made the holiday comfortable and pleasant for me. She often thought of her grandmother while making cakes and pies just the way she did while telling me what Christmas was like when she was little. Uncle Dawson went out into the woods and chopped a tree for momma and her cousin Dorothy. They put it in a bucket of ashes and pushed it into the corner of the living room. They made paper angels, stringed popcorn and made Santa's and reindeer from dough for the tree. They didn't have lights or Christmas balls and sometimes no presents.

There wasn't anything under the tree for me.

Wisdom and Faith

*I got a dress once and doll years later from my
mother. What made the holiday special was
gathering around the piano singing Christmas
carols and my grandmom's love for me. We had a
lot of fun at church and Lord knows we had plenty
of food. Most people didn't have much more than
us. Electric lights didn't come out until after the
war. Grandmom had a taste of her Christmas wine.
The old folks sipped it lightly, she wouldn't let 'em
have too much.*

I heard the phone ring. Then I heard
Momma say *"Oh no! When?"*
Funerals in Gwynedd, Penllyn, and Ambler
were long and drawn out. Even after I came along,
the old ways were still alive. As soon as word got
out that someone died, they came over the hill and
out of the fields to find out what happened. The
telephones were hot spreading the news. Momma
threw me in the back seat; dad was at the wheel
and up route 309 we went.
I remember when my Aunt Grace died. She
was my paternal great-aunt and the first funeral I
ever attended. My parents and I slowly walked up
to the west Ambler house with the crepe on the
door. Solemn faces greeted us in the quiet house
filled with people. They whispered greetings and
exchanged hugs in silence. The house reeked of
that sweet sick funeral flower smell mixed with
ham and biscuits. I heard someone whisper "Who
got the Body?" Ciavarelli and Hopson Reynolds

Wisdom and Faith

were the most respected and established undertakers. The cause of death was never spoken above a whisper and only privileged ears could hear. I looked for my usual seat in a corner somewhere in the living room. Among the mournful crowd was Aunt Grace laid out right there. Mom was standing behind me watching my gape. I never saw a body in the living room before. I decided to find a spot in the dining room instead. Piles of cards and people were all over the house. The house was filled with murmurs about how many car loads were coming up from Virginia; who was staying with whom and who going to preach the funeral.

The body stayed in the house every night until the funeral. The family stayed up all night. Every knock at the door brought more food; ham, turkey, mashed potatoes, turnip greens, corn, old southern rolls, cakes, pies, and that was before the repast. Big church sisters ate all night talking well of the dead. The family met at the house Saturday morning to line up with the limos. The funeral started at the usual eleven o'clock time and lasted about two, maybe three hours. I remember walking into the church watching mom sign the family book. Then she took my hand and we walked down the aisle toward the casket. The people in front of me slowed while taking their time to view the body. Some people touched her; others kissed her. I couldn't do either. Aunt Grace wore a soft blue shroud and blue slippers. Her long salt and pepper was wrapped in a bun nesting on top of her head. Her skin looked like plastic with a matte finish. I sat between my mom and dad on the second pew. From there I had a full view of the casket and the profile of Aunt Grace's head. Draped in black, the immediate family entered last. Everyone rose and didn't sit until Aunt Grace's children and Uncle Will were seated. The lid was closed just to and a spray was placed on top. One of the choir sisters stood to moan up Amazing Grace. It took at least fifteen minutes just to get the first two words out. I kept the obituary in my hand to follow the program, calculating how much longer the service would be. The eulogy wasn't much different than an ordinary service. The call and response brought a bitter confluence of salvation and grief. I knew when it was almost over when the undertakers marched down the aisle and removed the spray to open the casket for the final viewing. It was accompanied with *Precious Lord or Blessed Assurance*. It was the most emotional part of the service—long and heart wrenching. The children gathered around blocking my view, but momma said this was the last good bye. They covered their mother with a cuddly blanket and a sheer handkerchief over her face. That's when it got me. Their cries hurt and it gave me tears of my own. I held mommy's hand a little tighter as the undertaker closed the lid and that click rang out through the church. People fell on top of the casket in the futile effort to hold on. The

Wisdom and Faith

church sisters had to hold them back and have smelling salts on hand. I helped to carry the flowers out of the church and waited for my parents. Meanwhile my family greeted me. Some I knew, others only knew me as Hazel's child. Our car was a block down the road. We lined up to go to the graveyard where another service would take place ending with *I'll Fly Away.*

Most of our family is buried in Rose Valley cemetery on Butler Avenue in Ambler. The white folks are buried in Rose Hill cemetery right next to us. A cyclone fence draws the line. Lime and moss-stained headstones almost completely map the family.
Caskets were lowered into an over box, a caste iron casing with a lid, and the men of the family covered the grave with dirt using new shovels. I heard the sisters break out in tongue while others sobbed helplessly. I stood blank listening to that awful thud when the dirt hit the top of the over box. Mom was standing beside me reassuring me with her tender hug. She said it's where we all have to go; either you'll witness mine or God forbid I'll witness yours. But if you make your peace with the Master, there is nothing to fear. He'll see to it that we meet again in the eternal morning.

Nobody left until the over box was completely covered. Women wore black dresses and men wore a black guarder on their sleeve for one year after the death of parent or spouse. Then they went into second mourning wearing only black and white for six months.

Lower Gwynedd and Upper Dublin Township police escorted the procession from the church to the cemetery, then back to the church basement for the repast. There was more hugging and kissing at every turn. Old folks I never saw before in my life were so happy to see me. I took momma's lead and had a seat. After everyone settled in, the reverend blessed the table, the grieving family and the day, every slice of bread and every potato and finally us. The Missionaries had the kitchen hot. They busted out with the best food serving the immediate family first. I couldn't eat for passing food up and down the banquet table. Sitting elbow to elbow—butts brushed the back of my head knocking my hand and eye alignment totally out. I had to drop my head to get the fork to my mouth. If I had turned around, I could have kissed it, but I knew I had to act like I never saw anything.

One by one people left church and half of them headed to the family home for the rest of the evening. That's when the family got together to hash over the day. I knew when they were hashing because it was the only time they whispered. Then they were starting in on other peoples' funerals from years ago. They mapped out everybody in Rose Valley. They had to go over every single detail to find the lies and dirt—how loving the husband or wife was and how many children came from the union. Women huddled to share what they knew about what children didn't belong to which spouse but if fish got caught in their net that was their fish. Then come find out the couple wasn't married anyway. They remembered the day when the deceased did wrong—rough hombres or dirty heifers. They testified the hombres and heifers had to call on the same people they did wrong for help—the chickens came home to roost. I will never forget when somebody shouted, "You born baby, but you ain't dead and you don't know what black dogs' ass you gotta kiss before you meet your maker".

They stopped short of putting money on the table betting on who knew what. Momma said in the old days hardly anyone had obituaries. Most people couldn't read or write and many didn't even know their age. Some went to anybody's funeral just to see who was laid up and what could be found out then come home and talk about it. If a particularly notorious person died, it wouldn't be missed for the world. Nana and Aunt Ella were the worst. They viewed the body together—they looked down for a long time, shook their head, then look at each other. I saw what was coming on their face as they walked back to the pew.

Wisdom and Faith

"Homzell, did you see what they laid her out in? She wore dat dress to her momma's funeral. And what dey put all that makeup on her like dat for? She's too ugly for all dat bright red lipstick!" Aunt Ella looked at Nana like it was her idea.

"And the children ain't shed a tear. She was low for so long." Nana shook her head. Aunt Ella looked up "You either have to get well or die cause people get tired of you if you stay sick too long".

Nana and Aunt Ella hunched each other all thru the service. It kept the dining room table going for weeks.

The first time I ever heard about the Great Depression was from my mother. She was four years old when the stock market fell, five years after her grandfather's death. She had plenty to eat, did lots of hard work and heard stories about her grandfather, Shadrach. He worked from can't see in the morning until can't see at night until the day he died. Shadrach was a dark brown skinned man with a thick heavy beard. Nana said he had piercing eyes, a heavy voice and an evil streak. His life was hard work and God's word. He was especially hard on his daughters just short of being cruel.

"He walked through the house like Gawd walked the water." Nana was so proud to say. "When he walked down the road on Sunday morning for church, everybody jumped back! He was the top man. Oh pappy was something. He worked on the farm, at the flour mill down on Swedesford Road and had his shawl and hat ready on Sunday morning. His voice rattled the dishes in the cupboard! We couldn't move until he said so. Wasn't no drinking and cussing in pappy's house." Nana went on talking about pappy and what a hard strong man he was. I was scared of him just hearing about him and relieved we were not in the same lifetime.

After his death in 1924, Nana was just seventeen and became pregnant with my mother Hazel before his body was cold. She and Edward Johnson were married for about fifteen minutes.

Love and commitment meant nothing to the elders. If a young girl came up pregnant, she and the young father married. Their point was to give the child its rightful name. To them, it could only be properly done through marriage. In spite of their nuptials, neither Homzell nor Eddie meant each other any good. My grandfather, Eddie ended up taking a job as a Pullman on the railroad and Homey got a sleep-in job, a full time housekeeper, cook and laundress, in Jenkintown leaving their daughter Hazel Johnson with her maternal grandmother Luella Williams.

Mom was a cute but pitiful chocolate child with mostly wrapped, unkempt hair, a sweet personality and three dresses to her name, two for school and one for Sunday. Her orphaned heart was kept alive through her grandmother's love. She was born with a spirit that refused to be under anyone's control but her own. School and church brought music into her life and were the only two places where her song was welcome and brought relief from the isolation of Swedesford Road.

In 1931, mom and her cousin Dorothy attended The Springhouse School on Norristown Road which is now Gwynedd Mercy Academy. After feeding the chickens and having breakfast, they went across the field to Sumneytown Pike and Route 202 to catch the school bus across the street from the William Penn Inn to Spring House School.

Sometimes we had to walk pass prisoners

working on the roads. Chain gangs were right there—they were chained together wearing black and white striped clothes picking and digging. Big white men had guns keeping an eye on everything. Me and Dorothy looked right at the ground as we walked by. We stood as far away as we could, waiting for that ugly green school bus to take us to school. By fourth grade, I was a crossing guard on that same corner.

"You mean that busy intersection of Route 202 and Sumneytown Pike?" I figured momma had her corners mixed up.

Traffic wasn't like it is today. I wore a white strap that crossed my chest. First I had to line everybody up. Then I walked out into the street and put my hand up to stop the traffic and everybody crossed the street. You have to remember, this was 1935, we didn't have traffic lights and people weren't runnin all over top of each other like they do now. I loved it. It the only time I got to tell grown folks what to do.

They started the school day saluting the flag and singing songs like *Old Black Joe* and *My Old Kentucky Home* giving mom and Dorothy a deliberate second look when singing the verse *'it's summer where the **darkies** are gay'*. They read *Tar Baby* and *Little Black Sambo* and made music using pencils and empty boxes for instruments.

Springhouse School had two to three classes in one room with one teacher and ten to twelve children per grade. She took the time to teach each student in each class and didn't let anyone have peace until the lesson was learned inside out and upside down. Springhouse School had all white, college educated teachers. The all colored Penllyn School, only had a few college grads. A senior or tenth grader may be an elementary teacher. Despite this, lessons were learned thoroughly.

Many times the only lunch mommy had been a broiled sweet potato and a piece of corn bread, or a soggy jelly sandwich wrapped in a plastic bread bag. She felt embarrassed next to the little white children, mostly Quaker and Dutch, who had nice neat sandwiches wrapped in wax paper.

On Bethlehem Pike just down from Dager Road was an orphanage for colored girls called House of the Holy Child.

Before Brown vs. the Board of Education

Hazel Johnson, right with her cousin Dorothy at
Spring House School, 1932.

*They were considered waifs. People shunned
them. They went to Penllyn School with the other
colored children, but sometimes they came to
Spring House for final tests, but we weren't
allowed to talk to them and nobody talked about
them. During recess we had to play on opposite
sides of the yard. I know it was wrong, but the
times were as ignorant as the people. We used to*

call them the Home Girls which stigmatized them.

"If Penllyn was the colored school, how did you end up at Spring House?" I wondered.

Because I lived in Gwynedd. Colored folks lived in Penllyn. Penllyn is really the colored end of Spring House.

"Why was everyone so distant? Were they dangerous or ugly?" I asked.

The old folk figured they came from no account people otherwise they wouldn't be there. Just about all of them were from Philly. That was bad news right there—city folk. Nobody knew who they were and what they come from. That was enough to keep away from them. I saw them sometimes on Sunday at Brunson's store in Penllyn after church, but I never got too close. I remember one girl named Wealthy. She was so pretty and a nice girl. I liked her, but I knew I wasn't allowed to be her friend. Grandmom would've killed me.

Mommy called Momma Lou mom until she was about six or seven years old. Grandmom wiped her tears, soothed her pains and made her laugh all through her childhood. Luella's arthritic hands and swollen knees made it difficult sometimes for her to take care of her grandbaby, but she did the best she could. Her sometimes feeble attempt to love and care was just enough for her little Hazel. Mom didn't know Homzell was her mother until she was about six or seven years old. She was known as Aunt Homey to her cousins, so mom called her Aunt Homey too. It was one of her first reprimands. Homzell told her "I'm not your auntie, I'm your mother." How in the world was she supposed to know?

Shad and Lou's sons, Dawson called Dossy and George, were most like their father; tall, dark, average looking and hard working. The other brother, Elisha, called Lush, was a tall, black handsome man and married a pretty light-skinned woman, Aunt Nina. They both worked for the Hollingsworth family on Cow Path Road, now called Meeting House Road in North Wales. Mom often admired her uncle and how sharp he looked in his butler uniform with his cap and white gloves driving the Hollingsworth car, a black Pierce Arrow with wide white wall tires and bumpers made of solid nickel. Uncle Dawson was a hard working man but mom described him as mean and evil. He knew nothing of kindness but everything of working hard and saving a dime. Sometimes he was called Jesus Christ. Every time something happened the first thing out of his mouth was Jesus Christ!

It could be anything—a chicken died, somebody had another baby, a storm came up. He blessed me out for being Homzell's child, like it was my fault for being alive. I didn't even have a name. I was called that ole gal. I had nobody to go to except grandmom who was too old to defend me and needed Uncle Dawson and Aunt Rosie there to help her tend the farm. Then I saw him treat other people the same way, even his daughter. He made her life miserable too.

Elzina 'Nina' Williams Uncle Lush's wife 1930s

Uncle Dawson married Aunt Rosie from South Philadelphia. She was a tall red light-skinned woman with thick dark brown hair who was quick to jump salty on anyone. Their daughter Dorothy was first cousin to my mother and there they all lived in the Gwynedd home. Sometimes mom felt alone, like an outsider because Dorothy had her mother and father and my mother didn't. On more than one occasion Dorothy made sure mom didn't forget it either.

You know, after a while, you get tired of feeling bad. Then you get mad. That's when my big mouth was born and of course I was still wrong. I was outta place because I asked too many questions—a smart ass. Grandmom kept a lid on me because I was just a child, but I was quietly learning how to fight back.

Thanks to the Wall Street blunder, life was getting harder by the day. Hoover said that there would be a chicken in every pot and a car in every garage. Well, bullshit to that. It was more like chicken feet in every pot and they came from the backyard. Since there was no FDIC, people lost all of their money in the banks on that infamous October day, including Momma Lou. It was money 'Pappy' left for her after working for the Bigalow family and side jobs for many years. He left her five thousand dollars. It was big money for that time. It was all she had. Momma Lou, now an elderly widow, worried many nights along with millions of other people over the loss of her money, but she kept plugging along. "There's no

shame to be in the gutter" she'd say to mom. "With
the white man running this world it's out of your
hands. The shame is to wallow. There is always an
excuse for rags, but never for dirt." Mom told me
that even if I have nothing but orange crates for
tables, that's fine, just keep them clean and put
some roadside weeds in a jelly jar to make it look
nice.

*Many was the day we had to wash our
clothes at night and wear them again the next day.
We were ragged sometimes, but never dirty and
everyone was in the same pot.* Mom reminded me
while ironing one of the many dresses I had for
school.

Farming was long hard work. The plow had
to be hooked to the work horse to turn the dirt then
taken off and replaced with the harrow to break up
the soil. It had to be done two or three times to
make rows suitable for planting. It was done patch
by patch. Momma Lou and Aunt Rosie began
planting on the first patch while uncle Dossy
started the second patch.

*Uncle Dossy and Aunt Rosie had scythes to
clear the field. He started plowing between the
bottom of April and the top of May. We didn't have
our own horse. We had to get one from another
farmer, Mister Gibbs. Sometimes we had a mule.
Uncle Dossy hooked up the plow and walked
behind the mule. One day, I'll never forget it; the
mule got to fartin and let me tell you, there ain't
nothing worse than a mule fart. It took fifteen*

*minutes for him it get it all out. I could hear Uncle
Dossy way out in the field justa fussin. 'Jesus
Christ!' Dorothy and I fell out laughing. Ah Dossy!
Leave dat mule be! You know it gotta fought! That
was Aunt Rosie. I tell ya, there wasn't no birds
singing when that mule cut loose!*

Overturned dirt drew the prettiest birds from
all around. All the worms and grubs came to the
surface and the birds had a feast. The good earth
was rich and dark like chocolate. It made the air
smell sweet and clean. Mom reminisced about the
familiar smell of the country and the beautiful
birds that came to visit. The earth was clean and
pure. Mom and her cousin Dorothy trampled into
the woods where they took a drink of cold clear
water from running streams and shared its purity
with the frogs and tadpoles.

Sometimes the wonderful smell was cut
short when Mister Morris Queenan passed by in
his truck. Mister Queenan's job was to clean out
the cesspool for the few people who had plumbing.
When the truck was full, leakage oozed from the
back of the tank as it rolled down the road.

*We called it the honey dripper. That truck lit
up all of Gwynedd. One sniff was a firm reminder
that we're all the same.*

Mister Queenan started his business when
indoor plumbing was in its infancy and only the
rich could afford it. There was no municipal sewer
system and waste was flushed from the toilet into a
septic tank or cesspool. When these pools filled up,

they had to be emptied. Mister Morris owned his own home, fathered sixteen children and sent them all to college cleaning septic tanks.

Momma Lou hobbled to do farm work, housework and took in laundry. She wore a head wrap, long dresses with long sleeves even on the hottest day and high top button shoes. On about 35,000 square feet of land, from Route 202 to Sumneytown Pike to Swedesford Road, grandmom and Aunt Rosie planted turnips and corn, green beans and tomatoes, cabbage and carrots, peas and peppers. An asparagus bed was in the back of the farm.

Side view of the old house about 1930

Mommy and her cousins, 1930

Chopping wood, building fires, and pumping water started them off. Laundry day meant building a fire outside in a tin tub about as big as two people and putting the clothes in boiling water. Two tubs were needed to wash and rinse the clothes that were wrung by hand and sometimes a third tub of starch water for doing other peoples' laundry. No bleach, soap powders or cleaning liquid of any kind existed. The only way to whiten clothes was to boil them and stir them with a tree branch. Everything came out blinding white. With homemade soap from animal fat and lye, the shavings were put into the pot for soapy water. It had to be shaved to keep it from sticking to the clothes. That same soap was also used to clean the house and to bathe. Sometimes when grandmom ran out, she sent either Dorothy or mom to buy soap. They walked from Gwynedd to North Wales, about three miles one way to buy a bar of P+G or

Octagon soap. They dry cleaned wool blankets and coats by dipping them in a tub of kerosene, then hung them on the wire clothesline for a day or two.

Grandmom took in laundry from the white folks to make some money. She threw our clothes in along with theirs. Some folks wore the same clothes way too long before they were washed, especially in the winter. Nobody died; they were just a little funky sometimes. Right after Labor Day people put their long draws on and didn't take them off until spring. Women wore snuggies and men wore a union suit with the back door back or sometimes a split. The splits got plenty shitty. It buttoned up around the neck right down to the ankles. Funky folk were common and the worst place was in church.

Even I had to laugh at that one while remembering these people both black and white weren't trifling. It was a time when to take a hot bath meant that water had to be pumped and hauled, wood had to be chopped and a fire started to heat the water. Difficult to do in January with a house full of people, and so many other chores taking priority.

I remember my mother saving soap chips when I was little. When the bar became a sliver, in the jar it went. One rainy afternoon we were in the kitchen and she showed me how to make soap. It wasn't from scratch, just recycled. Mom took the jars of chips and put them into a large cooking pot with water on a low flame, stirring every once in a while. She stewed them down like she was making dinner. Soon the whole kitchen smelled like someone just had just taken a hot bath. While the soap was cooking she told me about the importance of not wasting.

I'm a Depression child and we didn't waste anything. We had to make do with what we had. Nothing was wasted.

All of the soap melted into a caramel goo. The coloring from the slivers was all boiled away. She let me stir the soap for a while warning me that hot soap is hotter than fire itself. With her instruction I poured the bubbling mess into a brownie pan where it had to cool. I wanted to know what all of this had to do with being a Depression child. What kind of child was that? I sat down watching the soap cool while mommy prepared chicken soup and a grilled cheese sandwich. The kitchen was quiet except for the patter of rain tapping at the window. It was just the two of us and she took me in—into her soul. She always could. She took me into her life. She made me a little girl in the thirties, seeing through her eyes and feeling with her heart exactly what it was like.

They were some hard times, but they weren't complicated. We didn't have the things people have now when I was your age.

She looked at me while pointing from the stove to the faucet, from refrigerator to the television and the telephone. I sat there quietly eating and listening.

During the week we just had wash-ups. Just enough to keep the funk away. The Saturday night bath in the tin tub was part of the weekly ritual to get ready for church the next day. It took a long time to pump and heat a tub full of water and it wasn't about to go to waste. Little kids went first and grown folks last. Only kids could take a sit down bath. Grown folks were too big for the tub. There were two pots going on the stove to keep heating the water as it cooled in the giant galvanized tub. After the lye soap bath, everyone greased down with petroleum jelly and during really hard times it was lard. Lard could have been anything. Once in a while it was from pigs, but it was usually mutton tallow. I think they call it lanolin now. Sometimes grandmom roasted a duck or goose for dinner and ya know they're oily. She roasted it on a rack and let the oil drip into a pan. That was good grease to mix with mustard powder, sulfur or asphedolene for colds. Aunt Ella lived in Ambler around the Italians and sopped her children down with olive oil. We didn't have toothpaste either. We used salt or baking soda as a dentifrice. Baking soda was a household staple for a lot of things; it was a deodorant, used for an upset stomach and for cooking. Old school flu shot was pot liquor—juice from the greens. It kept everyone regular and colds and the flu at bay or so legend has it. A nasty slug of Castor oil or Cod Liver Oil was a daily ritual. A petroleum by-

*product was coal oil and tar grease which was
used on hair to fight off ringworm and tetter which
is like cradle cap; it's thick oatmeal-like dandruff.
It comes from not having regular shampoos—
didn't have shampoo. When they did wash their
hair, it was with that lye soap that left people dry
and itchy. Black children as a rule didn't get head
lice that was more with white children. A good
dose of kerosene killed lice. Black children had
that tetter and ringworm. When women had their
menstrual cycle, there was no such thing as
sanitary napkins and forget tampons. We used
rags. Big thick rags. They were washed in the tub,
the same way as cloth diapers and used over again
and hung out to dry at night when nobody could
see. In the winter, they dried by the fire and the
house didn't burn down. When I became a teenager
there were some products out, but who could afford
it? I was working in the white folk's kitchen before
I got my first box of Kotex. It was like wearing a
mattress and I needed all kinds of pins and belts.
But at least I didn't have to wash rags anymore.*

*Grandmom used borax and lye soap to clean
the house. It was the same soap that washed our
bodies and clothes. We didn't have vacuums so to
get the dust and dirt out of the rug, we took it
outside and threw it over the wire line and beat it
with a broom. If it wasn't taken outside it was
swept with a wet broom to keep the dust down.
Nobody I can think of had wall to wall carpet.*

Beds had the bare metal spring. To keep bed

bugs away, the spring was taken outside and set on fire with kerosene to kill them. Windows were cleaned with kerosene or vinegar and water and the furniture was waxed with bees wax right from the hive and we coated the flat iron to keep it from sticking to the clothes. We had to improvise. It was the only way to make it. Food was in an icebox. A block of ice was clear as glass and there was a drip pan underneath to catch the drippins which was later used to wash clothes. There was no such thing as a freezer. The salt barrel kept meat from spoiling. Think you could live like that?

Mom's stories kept my mouth open. I thought about having to go to the coop to gather eggs then build the fire and get the water from the well and wait for it to heat before I could wash.

"Wow momma, how did you do all of that? Wasn't it hard? No toothpaste! Not even Johnson's Baby Lotion?" It was all beyond me. I couldn't imagine a time when people couldn't take a bath or had to make their own heat.

People need a lot of what money can't buy and very little of what money can buy. Folks don't understand that anymore. I did what I had to do. It was hard, everybody had it hard, but it was a good life. We had it better than most because the land sustained us. In some ways, it is better than today because we knew exactly where our food came from and the earth was still clean.

The next day I cut the soap into blocks and

wrapped it in wax paper. I couldn't wait to take a bath with my first batch of homemade soap. It didn't smell as good and was a lot softer than store soap, but it was a special bath that was made with our soap on one of so many special days. To think something like the soap I had in my hand was used to wash everything.

Every time mom washed aluminum foil to use over again, I thought about what she told me. I watched her pour water from boiled potatoes and string beans into the meat juice to make the gravy, how she always pre-soaked clothes and used Fels Naptha soap on shirt collars and the feet of socks and got busy on the scrub board while the Agro starch was cooking on the stove, adding bluing in the second rinse for white clothes. She used that same bar to scrub the kitchen floor for scuff marks before she washed it. She never used a mop for the floor, she got on her hands and knees until the floors were sparkling. Then she went back over it with a thin coat of Klear floor wax. When a jar of jelly, mayonnaise or anything was empty, she somehow could wipe a jar cleaner than anyone I know. It didn't matter how empty is seemed; she could always manage to get out just enough for one more sandwich. That comes from being a Depression child.

The laundry they took in had to be pressed with a heavy flat iron heated on the stove. Starch was slowly cooked on the stove and poured into the second rinse tub for stiff crisp shirts.

Pillowcases, tablecloths and shirts were made from pure cotton. There were no synthetic blends or fabric softener. They were ironed while damp making it easier to get the wrinkles out. "Careful with mistas shirts! I don't wanna see no cat faces in'em!" Momma Lou warned mom while she ironed after school. She taught mom how not to iron in wrinkles around the shoulder and get the collar crisp and straight and how long to keep the iron on the stove to go at it again. She kept a mucky sweat even in the winter standing on a stool to get the ironing done to grandmom's satisfaction and deliver back to the white family who paid fifty cents for the entire wash.

A slop jar was brought in the house every night and it was someone's job to empty it in the outhouse the next day. It had to be cleaned and aired outside for the next night. Newspaper and the Sears catalog served as toilet paper. Leaves off of the nearest tree did just as well. Children unaware of the dangers were vulnerable to using a poison ivy leaf to wipe their butt with predictable results.

The white folk's kitchen was where most black folks got their first taste of roast beef and learned what a capon was and mom was no exception. These well off families never ate leftovers. While many people were eating from the soup lines and apple carts, my family along with many other black families from the area ate top shelf leftovers.

Aunt Bert and Uncle Bill worked for a

private family. Aunt Bert was a working dog—
doing dinners almost every night of the week. She
prayed for eight days a week so she could work
more and make more. All she ever did was work
and save. She was a tall portly dark skinned
woman who was civil at best and out right ornery
at worst. Uncle Bill was soft spoken, brown
skinned man. He wore Ben Franklin glasses, loved
his cigar and had better honor and obey Aunt Bert.
They lived on Kerbaugh Street in Nicetown and
had a car, but took the train to work because they
were afraid to let madam and mister know they
had a car. White people didn't like uppity coloreds.
One of mom's first jobs was, of course, a maid.
She was an apprentice of sorts in the kitchen,
helping Aunt Bert get ready for the big dinner.
That's how she learned about elegant dining, how
to properly set the table, left hand service, place
plate setting, and the sequence of courses. The
household staff included an upstairs maid, a
downstairs maid, a chamber maid, a personal maid,
a cook, butler and chauffeur. The head maid was
dubbed *Chief Cook and Bottle Washer* because she
was boss over the rest of the staff and could do any
of the jobs in a pinch. In general it was a nickname
for anyone who at least in their imagination had
acquired a position telling other people what to do.

A formal dinner included place plate setting.
Mom told me it was just like the movies. Uncle
Bill announced each guest and took their hat and
coat. Mom was in her black uniform with the white

apron and the butler wore tucks and tails with a starched white linen cloth properly hung across his forearm in preparation to cater the meal. The protocol was to never have an empty place in front of the guest. It consisted of a large plate from which no one ever ate. Inside of the large plate was the dinner plate and on top of that was the bullion cup. It is a small cup with two handles. The flatware was hand polished Gorham silver found in local thrift shops now.

The tablecloth was beautiful linen with hand sewn detailing. To iron this massive cloth, a bed sheet was used on top to keep from ruining the delicate detail. The cloth had to be rinsed in starch water and ironed while damp. Wax was rubbed on the bottom of the iron to keep it from sticking from the build up of starch. It took two to three hours to complete one cloth with either a flat iron or a heavy electric iron. The table was set with this beautiful cloth and the matching napkins that had to be folded just so, and a bouquet of flowers to match the season.

The guests gathered in the living room with beautiful evening gowns and tuxes. The host and hostess greeted the incoming guest with well rehearsed behavior. It was a proper and polite evening chilled with fraudulent laughter and dangerous façades.

Course one, the bullion was served. Mom was instructed to always serve the madam first then proceed around the table. The madam led the protocol. If a guest wasn't sure about what to do, they were to follow the hostess. When the guests were finished, the cups were removed and the salad was served followed by a sorbet served in a lily shaped glass dish. The next course was dinner.

Food was never placed on the table in serving bowls. The dinner plates were stacked in front of the mister who carved the meat while the butler stood to his left. The butler served around the table starting with the madam and the uniformed maid served the rest of the meal to each guest from their left.

A buzzer was under the madam's foot that was connected to a bell in the kitchen. Under the bell was a panel with the name of the room where to report: Guest bedroom, dining room, parlor, and living room.

After dinner, the guests retreated to the living room where demitasse was served on a silver tray and placed on the coffee table. While they were enjoying themselves indulging in talking shop or sing-along's, the crew in the kitchen had all of the dishes, pots, pans, fine crystal and porcelain to wash. Mom's job was to help clean this lavish mess as if a dinner had never taken place. Everything had to be washed, dried and placed where it belonged. That beautiful tablecloth that took three hours to iron had to be done all over again, along with the napkins. Automatic dishwashers, dryers and washing machines belonged to the future. Only the ringer existed. The night may not end until midnight for the guests. That meant 12:30 AM or so for the help who still had to be ready to serve that three minute egg and toast in the morning so mister could catch the 8:03 AM train. And some had the nerve to call coloreds lazy.

Doing days' work was really the only way to make a living and it was more than trying. Maintenance of the upper class life depended on the black back, sometimes day and night. Momma Lou told mom if hard times ever came, go to the white folk's kitchen where she was assured food and shelter. She could always work to pay her keep. Sometimes household items the madam didn't want were an extra perk. It was how many people acquired beautiful and expensive dish sets and crystal. The only problem with that was sometimes The Madam, as she was called tried to get slick and use these items in place of pay. As a teen mom worked as a Mother's Helper on Saturdays. She cared for the new baby as well as the other children, washed clothes and helped prepare dinner and generally anything that was asked of her. At the end of the day, madam gave mom some clothes her daughter had outgrown. She came home to her grandmother who had a natural fit.

"You tic dem clothes right back over yonder and tell that woman to give you your money! That's how they cheat you. They give you what they don't want and keep the money too. Now ya done them two favors. Ain't no fattin frogs for snakes up in here." Momma Lou preached. "After a days work you get dat money and nothing else. Dem dresses ain't gone pay no tax bill or buy feed for the chickens!"

Momma Lou saved mom's money. She was allowed to keep maybe fifty cents and the rest was put away. One day she had twelve dollars in the jar. Momma Lou allowed mom five dollars with which she bought young girls stuff—perfume, make-up and a new deodorant called Mum. It was a thick white paste but a step up from baking soda. The white girls got jobs at the movies as ushers, popcorn girls at the five and dime store or the soda counter at the drug store. Colored girls had to work in someone's kitchen scrubbing floors or as a nurse maid for children.

Mom made three dollars and fifty cents a week doing different jobs. Picking a crop in the field for fifteen cents a basket was good money. Working for Hollingsworth farm, Johnson's farm and Evans family were considered respectable jobs. The Normandy's and the Wideners were the most prestigious families in the area, owning most of Gwynedd. Hollingsworth and Johnson farms were small private farms. Normandy was a big business dairy farm. Mom romped the grounds picking ox heart cherries and sometimes had a taste of their fresh ice cream. Colored people were not especially welcome at Normandy and it was understood not to hang around too much. There was a warmer reception at Hollingsworth and Johnson Farms.

Sleep-in jobs were as much as ten dollars a week with room and board. Servants had Thursdays off, known as Pot Slingers Day, and would visit family and friends. It was fairly easy to save some money, but trickery from some employers made it hard to keep. Miss Lily White was madam or any white woman of means. It was believed she knew everything there was to know about everything. Instead of the usual weekly salary of ten dollars, madam may offer eight dollars with the promise of investing the rest in a retirement fund. Colored folks didn't know anything about money beyond a stash in the mattress. But when Miss Lily died, the maid never saw one dime of that money. Whatever money that may have existed went to her heirs. Add up two dollars a week over the years plus interest. That was someone's pay never received; no retirement or dividend. It didn't always happen. Some people were very good to their help—set them up beautifully, but there were those who bore watching. Mom tucked that away in her wisdom account for future withdrawal.

Some colored people newly arrived in Ambler still had family in Virginia or North Carolina. Those who could would send money home to their family. Coloreds could not get checking accounts and sent cash through the mail. Their mother got the letter, minus the cash. They didn't realize that generational wealth was often generated by the theft and deception from the blood and sweat of the underclass. Mommy told me what the old folks told her as a girl. Many of them were slaves as children or their parents were for sure. They scornfully protested how everyone made money from their labor but them. Some of the worst ones behaved like the most devout Christians—strong on law and order, but never said too much about justice.

Northerners called people just up from the south Plum Nellie's—Plum out the country and Nellie in the city. They survived and got as far as they did depending on each other. Baby boys wore dresses the same as baby girls and these garments were passed from first one person then the next as babies were born. Gingham dresses made from feedbags were passed to those just coming up the road with nothing to wear. People gave from their heart looking for nothing in return except the hope of a better day through joint effort.

Once The Depression hit, everyone needed everyone else to survive. A knock at the door at any time may have been a hobo looking for something to eat. These transient people were trying to find their way just like everybody else. Grandmom happily prepared a meal for passers by: a piece of fat meat with stewed apples, biscuits and molasses and a cup of milk or maybe a cup of hot chicken stew. Grandmom never turned away a hungry belly, man or woman, black or white—

ever.

From the early days, Plum Nellie's reached the north, found a job in someone's kitchen and sent word for the next member. Most could not read or write and very few telephones were available. Their efficient grapevine got messages back and forth for families to reunite. Families slowly traveled north and squeezed in with kinfolk and through word of mouth eventually got a job or helped to farm the family land.

That's how Ambler got loaded down with Virginia. I wasn't around when it all began, but I remember every year there was another somebody up here from down the road. A house may have five people in it this year, by next year there were two more. The next thing you knew, the house was filled up with people. It was the only way to make it.

People opened their doors to strangers looking for shelter. Private homes were turned into rooming houses. People shared the house and sometimes clothes, food, money and yes, the man too. It was just a given that the landlord had free reign over the women under his roof. No one said anything, it was just understood. Some women were regularly sexually, physically and mentally abused without a second thought. It was a silent curse most had to live with. Then there were mommy's aunts.

Uncle Dawson's wife, Aunt Rosie, was not the one. They fussed and fought all the time. Aunt

Rosie thought nothing of cussing Dossy from Amazing Grace to a floating opportunity. She cussed him until she was out of breath. Then she had the nerve to ask the Lord to give her breath to cuss some more. That was because he was running around on her. She had a nerve because she was doing the same thing. One word brought on another. Dossy marched all over the house fussin at either Rosie or Jesus Christ. From what mom remembers, he was getting ready to meet his bitch this particular night and Rosie wasn't having it. She took an ice pick and popped the inner tubes on his 1935 Tin Lizzy—a Model T Ford. Then she told him to drive it. Rabid mad, he took a tray out of the steamer trunk and came down on Rosie's head. Blood flew and so did mom. All of this carrying on was going on under Luella's roof, who did nothing but go to her room and close the door. She was an old woman who couldn't handle that kind of upset. She didn't like those words either.

After uncle Dossy milked the cows, I had to make butter. I had to let the milk sit until the cream came to the top. Grandmom got mad at me if she caught me eating it— ain't anything sweeter than fresh cream. I lifted the cream out of the milk bucket and put it in another bucket to churn. Churning beats the cream into butter. It took about fifteen, maybe twenty minutes. Then I had a big ball of butter. I had to lift the butter out of the bucket to separate it from the buttermilk and then wash the butter. It had to be washed in ice cold

*water. That allowed any traces of milk to leech out.
If you don't, your butter gonna be sour. Buttermilk
was saved for making bread and biscuits. The
wash water was thrown out. The left over cream
was good to mix back in the milk or make delicious
ice cream.*

Grandmom made bread with coarse flour
from the flour mill in Flourtown, PA. It had to be
sifted three times to get it light and fluffy. A bit of
yeast was shaved off from a small block and
melted down then mixed with buttermilk. She
kneaded the dough until it would pop and blister.
Then she put it in the loaf pan. It was left overnight
in the warmth of the kitchen to rise. The next day it
was kneaded again and it would puff and blister
some more. The last time she kneaded it, she
would baste it with a brush full of melted sweet
cream butter and put it in the oven. It lit up all of
Gwynedd. She added some homemade apple or
pear jelly or molasses with strick-a-lean, a cup of
coffee or a glass of milk and that was a weekday
breakfast. They lived and ate well—close to the
earth. Nothing was wrapped in plastic, frozen or
processed. They didn't get sick and there wasn't
much cancer or diabetes or obesity. They didn't die
until they were old and ready.

*Everything comes in male and female, even
the vegetables. The male leaves of any vegetables
like collard, dandelion, doesn't much matter are
strong and bitter. The female plant is much tastier
and the leaf is tender. Broad dark green leaves are*

male. Now, on the farm the bull has one purpose, to make babies. If a young male calf was altered, he'll grow up to be a steer beef and it's the best beef to eat. Sometimes the calves were slaughtered too, that's where your good veal comes from. That's because they were milk fed; never ate food. We had turkeys, geese and ducks for Thanksgiving, but never the Tom.

The aristocrats loved to dine on the loin of beef. They had mint sauce with lamb, orange marmalade with roasted duck and raisin sauce with beef tongue. Coloreds ate whatever was left over. They were laughed at for eating greens, fish, watermelon and chitterlings. In the minds of some whites it was good enough for the niggers. Everything coloreds ate was debased as if it was garbage or eating grass that was meant for the porridge of cows and goats. The most nutritious food comes from mother earth like dandelion, collards, kale, mustard and yams. Fish was cheap and plentiful.

It seems odd how the very foods we were picked and poked and teased for eating are now not only 'officially' nutritious, but some, especially fish is difficult to afford. There was fine dining on the pancreas from pigs—sweet bread. Meanwhile, colored people ate pluck soup made from pig lung, heart and liver. Mountain oysters were testicles. Yea that's right, we ate them too! Nothing was wasted.

Mom sat back and thought about how all of

that went down. She told me that a moral authority prevailed in giving the most downtrodden people the most nutritious food. That's why our great-grandmothers could work in the field nine months pregnant in the heat of July. Mom remembered when she was working as a Mother's Helper, waiting on the little dainty who had to stay off of her feet and get total bed rest before the baby was born, eating soft boiled eggs and toast with a cup of tea.

She needed some side meat and corn bread washed down with pot liquor. She'd be alright then.

Momma Lou got honey right from the beehive. Mom loved to watch her from inside of the house. Grandmom walked across the field and fearlessly extended her arm into the gentle swarm. She slowly and gently put her hand inside the hive while bees covered her entire arm and buzzed around her head. She slowly got a glob filled with honey, the comb, and the wax. With a slower and gentle retreat she sloughed the bees off of her arm and they gathered to the hive again. Leftover bees were on her back and in her hair on her walk back to the house. Not once was she ever stung during her honey reaping venture. She treated them patience. She brought the honey into the house and drained it with a piece of cheesecloth over a mason jar. It took a few days for it all to drain. Mom said she loved to chew on the wax. Homemade biscuits and gingerbread were made with a dose of fresh honey right from the bees behind. That's why momma laughs now when people talk about eating organic food like it's something new and privileged. She has a field day on the Health Check where the new discovery was matter of course long years ago like the benefits of exercise called work in the old days.

That's what happens when you forget your history—or it's taken from you. Organic was all we had. Solid food was all we knew. You have these highly educated people rediscovering old stuff that the dispossessed have always known. They were ignored along with anything that was apart of them. Now here they come talking like its some brilliant revelation.

At times there were three hundred chickens. At least half of them had fresh eggs ready for the girls unless they were molting. Sometimes mom was just in time to see one starting to hatch. A freshly hatched chick was a loveable ball of dust after it dried. They were so cute and warmed mommy's heart. She was so taken away by them, Momma Lou had to come out to the coop and grab her so she wouldn't be late for school.

Sometimes chickens didn't lie until late in the day. I had to be careful not to get spurred by the rooster or pecked by the hens. We had Rhode Island Reds, Leghorn, and Dominick and Ban tons. Rhode Island Reds laid big brown eggs. They were corn fed—Golden Banner. Grandmom ground the corn coarse for the hens and fine for the baby chicks. When it came time to get one, either grandmom clipped her wing or she had to chase her down, sometimes I did too. Grandmom came down on that chicken with one chop. The chicken went one way and her head went the other way. Uncle Clarence was terrible. He didn't chop them—he rung their neck and you could hear that neck snap, just like that! A large pot of hot water was always on a low boil on the back of the stove. They scalded and plucked her clean. Sometimes when grandmom gutted the chicken, eggs were still inside. They plopped her in a pot of salt water to drain the blood and fried it up in that black iron footed frying pan—we called them spiders. That was the freshest chicken ever to eat. The meat was sweet and tender—just fell of the bone and taste like butter, um. We stuffed feed bags with down for pillows.

Once in a while a chicken got sick and died. Certainly can't eat him so the children got together to for a respectful funeral. Mom's cousin, Clarence Junior nicknamed Brother, got Shadrach's shawl and hat out of the attic and the girls were the choir. They found a cardboard box to use for the coffin. Dorothy and Ethel put rags over their head for a veil. Mommy got some weeds out the field and called them flowers. They sang and preached over the body. Uncle Clarence played along and gave the eulogy mocking a reverend who couldn't preach.

"I knowed her…Knowed her well…Knew

her mother and father…"

"Worked wit her….Ate her eggs…Knew her Chilin… Cleaned her coop…"

The girls moaned, Uncle Clarence preached and the boys played pall bearers and dug the grave. Then, after the funeral, was the repast. They ate biscuits and sang at their backyard table, '*Just a Closer Walk with Thee*' but with slightly different lyric.

Just a bowl of black eye peas…
Pass the biscuits if you please….
SALT AND PEPPER MAKES ME SNEEZE!
Just a bowl of black eyed peas!

Mom loved the piglets too. With their curly cue tails running around, squeaking and anxious to play, she indulged them. There were about five or six pigs on the small farm. During mating season, Momma Lou negotiated with Johnson Farms or Mister Enick Gibbs who had a boar to mate. The negotiation was either ten dollars or his pick of the litter when the piglets arrived. Since there was little money, the farmer agreed to a few piglets. He brought his prize stud to mate with the sows for about a week. After the babies were born and weaned from their mother, Luella kept half and gave the other half away. The mother was slaughtered for the kitchen table in late fall, and the little pigs replenished the farm.

Pig killing time was sometime after

Thanksgiving. Uncle Dossy had a machete about as long as your arm. He sharpened it on that whetstone until sparks flew. Just the slightest touch would cut you. Grandmom would yell at Dorothy and me,

"Yawl chilin get out the way!"

She didn't have to tell me twice. Mister Gibbs cut her head off in one swipe. Then Uncle Dossy slit her belly open. Dorothy and I flew. I didn't like it. It was a bloody mess. They had a wash tub to catch her guts. It looks cruel now, but at that time it was a matter of eating or starving. After they gutted her, she was hung on a tree to freeze her out for about a week. You got to get the worms and that animal taste out otherwise it will taste terrible. Green meat will kill you. The colder it was outside the better.

She was sewn up with burlap. We had a fire pit in the back. The men folks got that fire just right. Uncle Dossy poked the skewer through the mouth and it came out through the butt. Me and Dorothy used to blow up pig bladders like balloons and chase the cats up the tree. She roasted all day with a large bucket of barbeque sauce and a clean mop. Some of Uncle Dossy friends came by to help mop that sucker down, drink corn near the barn and play cards. The women were in the house all day picking turnip greens, frying chicken, whipping up potato salad and cleaning chitlins. By dinner time, the meat fell off the bone. Tender! Um!

Grandmom fried ham in the spider pan. She

broiled the sweet potatoes until the syrup oozed out of them. Talk about something good. She cut up apples and stewed them with the skins and added sugar, ground vanilla bean, a clump of butter and cinnamon. Add a pan of biscuits and some turnip greens and that was dinner.

Stewed or jarred fruit was for any meal or just a snack. Grandmom got one of the older chickens and prepared her for a slow stew, which was most of the day. If she saw someone walking down the road, which was often, she added another cup of water to the stew.

Everyone got up the table with greasy mouths and full bellies, picking their teeth with a straw from the broom.

They had all kinds of birds for Sunday dinner; chicken, duck, goose, squab or pheasant. They served ham with green beans, turnips and turnip greens, mashed potatoes, sweet potatoes and corn with buttermilk biscuits and cornbread made from meal. Nobody ate until the men were seated and served. Sometimes Reverend Edwards and his wife came to break bread and the best was set for them.

Pastors didn't make a lot of money. To survive, they made the rounds to all of the families for dinner that honored having them. The one thing everyone had plenty of was food. The evening usually ended about 8 p.m. after a taste of homemade ice cream and cake. The best cakes in the world were made from these ingredients with fresh vanilla right from the bean, fresh-churned butter, warm eggs right from the chickens' behind and fresh milk.

The smoke house was out by the hen house, which was beyond the outhouse. Stripped hickory and maple wood smoldered all winter seasoning slabs of meat, sausage and pork butts. Sage, basil and thyme from the garden were ground to a powder and mixed with scrap meat and put through a huge meat grinder that was fastened down at the end of the table. The rest of the meat cured in the salt barrel in the cellar where cabbage brewed to sauerkraut and kept the cellar smelling like a fart. But it was the best tasting sauerkraut with sausage and biscuits.

Something was cooking or brewing everyday. The smell of food was everywhere. Food was a favorite past time because there really wasn't much else to do. People couldn't afford the movies, many didn't have radio and of course no one could go anywhere. Travel wasn't a priority except for maybe a visit down to Westmoreland which was a big deal.

Chemicals didn't cure the meat, the cold did— along with salt and smoke from tree bark. Fat children were rare. One reason was the hard back-breaking work that was that required to get through the day. People walked to where they had to go. It was nothing for someone to walk from Gwynedd to Penllyn, or maybe from Gwynedd to Ambler. Short cuts through the fields were about ten to twelve miles one way. Uncle Clarence walked from Germantown to Gwynedd to see his mother. That's about twenty miles each way. Sweets were a treat and even they were homemade. People fell victim to childhood and community diseases—tuberculosis, diphtheria and whooping cough, which momma said was cured by taking the child to the outhouse and holding their head just above the hole. Children were vulnerable to pinworms. They were given a laxative, prunes or flax seed tea to wash it out of their system. In spite of no indoor plumbing or sanitation as we know it today, none of the family died from food poisoning. They hardly had upset stomachs. Fat, salt and sugar was a diet staple, but they still managed to live to be plenty old. Mom said some people actually ate lard sandwiches.

It got just that bad for some. The menu was oatmeal, cornmeal or no meal. Some folks took to a western sandwich which was two pieces of bread with the wide open spaces.

Everyone was talking about Joe Louis. The champ was the best thing that happened to coloreds since Reconstruction and Uncle Dawson had to get a radio to keep up. It was electric and sat in the dining room. The deluxe floor model played 78's and cost twenty dollars, about two weeks pay.

Uncle Dawson invited the guys over to listen to Joe Louis' big night. He was going at it with Max Schmeling. He was kicking ass. Tiddums Queenan and Mister Enick Gibbs sat around the dining room table and dared anyone to talk. When Joe won that night it was like New Years Eve and was when mom first heard Duke Ellington, Billie Holiday, Benny Goodman and Count Basie. Billie Holiday was her favorite because she could easily feel and identify with her hurt and pain. Billie's voice was strange but haunting. *God Bless the Child* changed her world forever. *Saint Louis Blues* set her on fire, but she had to keep it low because the 'raggedy music' was not especially welcomed in the Christian home. Grandmom didn't like it, but she let mom listen to it sometimes. She kept it low and kept her bounce to herself.

Momma and Aunt Rosie loved Bing Crosby. He was like Frank Sinatra back then. I could hear them singing along; bum, bum, bum, bum, bum. Aunt Rosie had a victrola she kept in her room. Grandmom was a deaconess at church. She had no liking for it at all—devil music. I listened, but when she came in the room, I just turned it off.

The family now enjoyed the luxury of radio after dinner. Everyone gathered to talk and sometimes listen to the evening news hoping for some relief from the hard times. They sat around enjoying a dish of fresh homemade ice cream and listened to the soaps on the radio like *Stella Dallas* and *The Guiding Light, Inner Sanctum, Mr. Keene 'Tracer of Lost Persons', Hilltop House* and *The Squeaking Door.'* Only AM radio existed; WIBG, WCAU and WPEN. Momma loved them. She worked hard all day so that privilege wouldn't be taken from her. The most popular commercials were for Barbasol shaving cream, Ex-Lax, and Lux soap. Radio signed off at 11 p.m. Long before that hour, grandmom looked at my mother and Dorothy dead in the eye, then looked at the grandmother clock in the hall. She never said a word. The two girls excused themselves and went upstairs to bed. That was successful discipline. There was no need for talk or action by anyone.

In those days it was common to go inside the house and hear nothing but people talking. There was no radio, television, telephone or record player.

Talk about quiet. You could hear a mouse piss on cotton. The only noise anyone had was the noise they made. Everyone had a piano and someone in the house could play it. That was about it. On a rainy or snowy afternoon there was absolutely nothing to do, I mean nothing at all. You just stared at each other all day long. The only book in the house was the Bible. I had a few books when I was older, but for the most part it was really hard to get through those days. If the tube blew, we didn't have radio for a while. We were not allowed to play cards and we didn't have games. I did some sewing or ironing and helped with dinner. So to walk into someone's home and hear the radio going was a spectacle. People were impressed and the word got around. Everyone sooner or later

*came by to listen to the radio. It didn't matter what
was on. I heard people talk about it at church.*

"They got a radio!"

"Get out of here! How they come by that?"

*"Well you know he works, he must make
good money" You know how people talk.*

*Then we got a telephone! It had a separate mouth
piece and speaker. It had to be cranked to make it
work. When the mouthpiece and the receiver were
one piece with a cradle to rest it on, oh Lord!
People really had a lot to say then.*

'They got the kind of phone, you know..."

No what are you talking about?

*You know the kind of phone with the mouth and the
ear all hooked up together?*

No, no I don't know anything about that.

*You don't even have to crank it. All you do is pick it
up and talk.*

*Go way! Really! Lord ain't that something! Sounds
like something my madam would have.*

People came to see it and learn how to use
it. To reach someone, the phone had to be wound
up and the operator would come on "What number
please?" then caller responded "Ambler 1234".
The operator answered "Hold the line please."
Some of the exchanges for Philadelphia were
Ratcliff, Ogontz, Freemont and Poplar. Fewer
people had to holler across the field or send
children across town to deliver a message. Good
gossip, sickness and funerals didn't have to wait.

Saturdays were the day Momma Lou and

Aunt Rosie got together to cook up their usual
cuisine. My grandmother, Homzell was there
adding fuel to the fire as usual and catching up on
gossip. She looked and smelled wonderful,
wearing nice clothes and new shoes—the same
things mommy needed. Grown folks talk was not
for young ears, but when mom could and even
when she wasn't supposed to, she stretched her ear
from the shed kitchen and heard a lot of dirt
slinging about people from Ambler to Fort
Washington. They went through everybody.

There were times my mother was ridden
with resentment when her mother came to see her.
Aunt Rosie seemed to love to watch her niece,
Hazel catch hell. Every time Rosie saw her sister-
in-law, she had a whole bucket of everything
mommy said or did. Of course, Nana put on a
show, hollerin and carrying on at mom—gave her
hell long enough to satisfy Aunt Rosie. After all it
was Rosie who was there with my mother, not
Homey. Aunt Rosie did mom's hair and cooked her
food so Nana couldn't say anything
otherwise she might end up stuck with her.
Sometimes Momma Lou put a stop to all the
carrying on. Forbidden to say anything put
mommy's brain in high gear. She took in how they
talked people down all the time. According to
them, everybody was a bucket of shit. After they
ravaged everybody in town, they started digging in
the church people. One of the deacon's was going
after the young girls. He supposedly got one of

them pregnant. Mom knew both the girl and the *respectable* old church man.

That's what got me out with a lot of those old folks. They were so full of dirt themselves and talked about people who were doing the same they were doing—then lie about it—and have the nerve to tell other people about their idea of right and wrong. They didn't know the meaning of the word friend. They stabbed anybody in the back. That's what grandmom didn't like. She told me about people who stand at your back and see your face well bruised. They were all pissing out of the same quill.

Canning began in August to prepare for winter. Mom and Dorothy's job was to pick tomatoes, green beans, corn from the garden and gathered up peaches, pears, berries and apples. All of the fruits and vegetables were washed, stewed, blanched and prepared for canning in Ball glass jars. Apples sat out until they were almost rotten to make apple cider. Luella and Aunt Rosie had jars and lids boiling in a large footed cast iron kettle pot. They built the fire high and had fruit, vegetables and jars boiling all at the same time.

This was in the middle of August. You know these people today would have all passed out with no air conditioning. Sometimes we caught a nice breeze. When it was hot it was just hot and we dealt with it. Hard, but not complicated.

With toggles holding the jar the food was

quickly canned and sealed. Skins from peaches, apples and pears were put together making Applejack. It was clear liquor. After the peelings worked in the barrel for awhile, it built sudsy foam on the top. The foam was skimmed off and the liquid was siphoned into another barrel and allowed to work some more until the liquid was clear. This green toxic liquor was put into an aging barrel that was smoked with hickory. After a time it was bottled and ready in time for Christmas.

Grandmom made mince meat and rhubarb pies. I didn't like either one of them. Mince meat is just what it says, ground meat—ground lamb mixed with lamb fat and apples and raisins. Rhubarb grew out in the field. You could never eat it as is. It would drive straight up the wall. It had to be stewed down with sugar and molasses.

Aunt Bert and Uncle Bill went to Florida every winter with the white people. They sent a large fruit basket up to grandmom with a picture of them in front of an orange grove. It was the first time we ever saw one. One of the fruits was quinces. They look like peaches, but they're not. They're sweet and delicious. Grandmom made preserves out of them.

Sarsaparilla was made by boiling sassafras root in a large pot. Licorice from the drug store and a little sugar was added followed by melted yeast. It was placed in the window sill where the sun worked the yeast. The foam was skimmed three times and cooled, then poured into dark brown bottles and capped. The bottles were placed in a tin tub with ice cold water. Mom remembered how full of flavor it was, tasting the ice cold strength and purity in every ingredient. Birch tree bark was stripped and slowly boiled to make homemade birch beer. Mommy used to like to suck the strong and tasty sap from the raw bark.

Nothing went to waste. Every kind of peel imaginable from potatoes to apples was used to make wine. Everything was homemade—beer, root beer, sarsaparilla, potato wine, dandelion wine, you name it they had it and they made it. Waste from fermenting fed the pigs or became compost. When the next door neighbors had the still going, the air smelled like toast bread. This could be a dead give away because it was during prohibition. That's why it was called moonshine; it was made by the light of the full moon. The still was located way out in the field between Swedesford Road and Route 202. If the children were caught back there it was hell to pay for sure. Didn't have to worry about the cops too much. Charlie Whistler was the head cop of Lower Gwynedd and told the man next door, Frisbee, not to worry. Just keep it cool, don't let anyone get out of hand tonight or he'd be busted. Of course, Whistler always had his quart for good measure. Flooky was the chief in Ambler and kept quiet as well. He just stopped by to get a little taste. Uncle Dossy made sure he stayed on good terms with Frisbee. When the still was dry next door, Uncle Dossy and Uncle Lush went to

Cathead's in Coal Point.

*They called it Coal Pint. Cathead ran a
good time house and always had a jug or two. The
men folks trucked over there to get a jug or two
when they were going to have a party. People had
to be careful where they got their liquor. Some
people sold bad liquor and it killed a lot of people.
Everyone had their connections just like today.*

Uncle Dossy took the plows off the horse
and took the kids out for a hayride. He'd get out
the buck board and away they went. They picked
apples off the tree for pies and cider and sang
songs along the way. The rest of the apples were
wrapped in newspaper and placed in a barrel where
they stayed fresh all winter long.

When money was tight, Nana and Aunt
Rosie had a party to pay the taxes and Lysters.
Lysters sold kerosene by the gallon, coal by the ton
and wood by the cord. They were three days
cooking getting ready for these parties. Uncle
Dossy had the liquor lined up and roasted a pig.
The women were busy in the kitchen. Aunt Rosie
came from a family of cooks. She had the best
apple pies and chocolate cakes.

Women didn't have makeup. Park and
Tilford makeup was too expensive. Besides it only
came in one or two different shades. Some black
women tried to wear it to make themselves lighter
looking like they had baking powder on their face.
Straw from the broom gathered soot from the stove

to line their brows and lard or petroleum jelly kept it in place. Lipstick doubled as rouge. The butt end of a butter knife curled their hair and, if they were really in a pinch, a fork to straighten it.

At the Saturday night party, Mister Morris Queenan, the honey dripper driver, was happy to sit in the corner and enjoy watching others enjoy. "Yall gone and hab a good tam." He had a heaping plate nearby. Mister Morris kept the peace. If anybody got a little too liquored up, he held his shotgun shouting "Anybody wanna go to hell tonight?"

The house was packed. It was fifteen cents to get in the door. Clarence's daughter Vivian collected the money. Mister Earl Gant sat at the roller piano playing *Darkness on the Delta* or plucking out some stride rhythms with a cigarette hanging from the corner of his mouth and a shot of corn under the piano. A full plate was fifteen cents and a little taste in the back room was a quarter. By and by, when the liquor took hold somebody broke out in a Buck dance or maybe grabbed a partner to Mess Around or Shim Sham. They had it hot. Men folks stuck in a corner telling dirty jokes while women were doing what they usually do, talking about everybody in there. Aunt Rosie had kitchen patrol and kept track of the money. While the party was going strong, Whistler and Flooky stopped by to check things out, got a plate of food, maybe a taste and kept on going. Mom and Dorothy had their eyes on top of their forehead watching grown folks carry on...

Did you see Miss Hudson?
Her husband wasn't with her.
Yea he is! I saw him over there. He's
dancing *with that other lady.*
Look at em go!
The entire house rumbled with foot stomps and
hand claps. Sometimes it was hard to hear the
piano with all the laughing and talking going on.
Then they took to singing everything from Bessie
Smith to gospel. They kept on going until daylight
tapped them on the shoulder. Some people kept on
going from the party right to church.

By tax day they had three hundred dollars. It
was a happy day in Gwynedd. Aunt Rosie got her
cut and so did Nana. They both had big bosoms
and kept the money wrapped in a rag and tucked in
their cleavage. Luella was able to pay her twenty
seven dollar tax bill and the coal company, and
saved the rest for the tax bill next year. She didn't
dare go to the bank. She stashed it in a strong box
in the plank of the floor underneath the bed she
shared with mom. Grandmom didn't like that
carrying on, but when The Depression came
around, everyone had to make a nickel the best
way they could. Very few homes were dry. Liquor
was on hand to sell and trade and of course for
medicinal purposes. Although prohibition was over
in 1933, it was one of many ways families
survived.

1934

Taxes in Lower Gwynedd Township
Montgomery County, Penna.

Floyd Schneider, Tax Collector,   Box 39, Gwynedd Valley, Pa.

M   Shadrack Williams, Est.

Gwynedd, Pa.

Bills must accompany remittances and stamped envelope for receipt.

Property assessed $ 1500.00
Occupation " $ } $ Road Tax 5 mills $ 7.50

Rebate 5% if paid before June 1st, 1934 $

Penalty 5% if not paid before October 2nd, 1934 $

Received Payment $

Electric Light Tax on $, at   mills $
Rebate, 5%, if paid before June 1st, 1934 $

Penalty 5% if not paid before October 2nd 1934 $

Received Payment $
Property assessed, $ 1500.00   School tax, 10 mills $ 15.00
                                    Per capita tax $3.00 $
No discount on School Tax
Penalty, 5%, if not paid by October 2nd, 1934 $

Received Payment $
Poll Tax $, 50 cents $
No discount on Poll Tax
County Tax on $ 1500.00   , 3 mills $ 4.50

Personal Property Tax on $, 4 mills $
Rebate, 5%, if paid before July 30th, 1934 $

Penalty, 5%, if not paid before November 2nd, 1934 $

Received Payment $

I will be at the following places and dates to receive taxes:

September 5, 1934   **September 6, 1934**
William Penn Inn, 9 to 10 A. M.   Gerlons Store, 9 to 10 A. M.
Cressman's Store, 10 to 11 A. M.   Rosenberger's Store, 10 to 11 A. M.
Magargal's Store 1 to 2 P. M.   Fraskenfield's Residence 1 to 2 P. M.

All taxes are delinquent after December 31st, 1934.

My mother started Ambler High School on

Tennis Avenue in1938. She sang in the glee club, took tap dancing and wrote the school song.

I sang at every Christmas recital. My favorite was O' Holy Night. I sang Italian songs like Italian Street Song and Come to the Fair and my favorite— the Ava Maria. Once I got home, I had to stop it. It wasn't embraced. They only thing grandmom was interested in were for me to bring in some wood. I loved the song It All Comes Back To Me Now. I changed the lyrics and made it our school song. My teachers told me I should consider the arts and develop my talents. They tried to encourage me to see a bigger world like the theater, but I knew my family would throw it out the window for me, so I didn't bother.

Mom couldn't wait to get to the dances that were held in downtown Ambler and Norristown with her friends. Everyone was raving about the upcoming dance and the big names of the day like Louis Jordan, Count Basie and Nat King Cole. She heard this great music on the radio and couldn't wait to get to the dance to hear live music. She had to put her reservation with grandmom first. She was all day trying to get up the nerve to ask her grandmother a week or two in advance if she could go.

"I'll see". . That was all she had to go on with a little more than a prayer, and no back talk about it either. Mommy walked on eggs. She got up extra early Saturday morning and slopped the pigs, collected the eggs, cleaned the coop, bailed the water, emptied the slop jar, brought in the wood, built the fire and anything else in hopes her grandmothers heart would soften. Well, Saturday night finally rolled around and thanks to prayer, she could go... after the lecture.

"Gal, you keep dat dress down! Keep dat red rag in your mouth! Don't you go out here half naked, you'll catch you a death of cold."

Mom and Dorothy were upstairs getting dressed for the dance. Mom had her dress ironed and starched and hair done. She had taken a bath earlier in the day and wore her best perfume, *Tweed.* She came down the steps so proud and pleased only to be greeted by Aunt Rosie.

"Gal, you sure don't have no shape. Ump. You just as flat chested as you wanna be."

Mom's smile died and her heart sunk. Then she was pissed.

"There's my gal!" Dorothy had just come downstairs.

"See, Dorothy has a shape, she looks good in her clothes. She don't look like a grass sack bag."

You know when Aunt Rosie got finished with me, I thought I was deformed. I had no titties, ugly legs and no shape, just not fittin to live. I couldn't talk back, but I learned not to pay her any mind at all.

Grandmom had mom in frumpy flannel wraps and boots to wear to the party. She had to wait until she was out the door to shed those old folk's clothes. "Leb'n clock! That's it! I ain't pot gutted over this no how so you better tic care!"

Norristown was the hot spot. She and her crowd ran on Violet Street and to Russell's on Maple Street. They stomped to Nat King Cole and Jimmy Lunsford. Everyone Lindy Hopped to *Tuxedo Junction* and *Central Avenue Breakdown*. Mom bounced home well after midnight and knew there would be hell to pay for staying out so late. Nobody locked their doors and windows, so she opened the living room window at the front porch because the door was squeaky. So far, so good. She went through the hallway to the bottom of the steps counting them as she went along because she knew the ninth step had an awful creak that woke everyone in the quiet of night. She miscounted. The step creaked.
"Gal! Is dat you?!"

Sometimes mom was allowed to keep company on Saturday afternoons. A young man knocked on the front door calling on one of the girls.

All they could do was show up. We didn't have a telephone. I answered the door and grandmom was right there. She had to know who he was and who his people were. That's how she decided whether or not he was fit company. That's why the old folks didn't like outsiders—people from Norristown and Philly. They didn't know what kind of lies and trouble were coming in.

Mom and her young man sat in the living room and grandmom sat in the dining room giving him the once over looking right down their throat and hearing everything they said.

There wasn't much to talk about. It's kind of simple now that I look back on it. The boy may talk about something in church, how nice our tomatoes were, what big chickens we had—maybe his sister cooked dinner the other day, but it was better when his grandmother cooked. I might talk about something in school or that big storm we had. There wasn't anyplace to go and nothing to do. Pitiful, ain't it? But that's what it was. That was keeping company.

When the clock struck eight thirty, maybe nine o'clock, grandmom had no qualms.

"Young man, times' gettin on. Bout time you got your hat and coat and get your horse and buggy or however you got here and get on."

There was nothing to say but "Yes maam."

Momma Lou's criticism was at its best when it came to screening mommy's potential beaus. She didn't like them too dark. Lots of folks were hung up on complexion. It was the responsibility for every grandchild to lighten up the family. She didn't trust light eyes, but liked light skin with a gold or yellow hue, but never red. Red rhiny Negroes were supposed to be evil and sneaky. Mom was warned to watch them.

"But momma, the Williams family is dark skinned themselves. Why would they snub other brown folks?" It was pure nonsense to me.

That comes from way back. Black folks can be just as prejudice as white folks. They always sucked up light skin and pretty hair. They never considered the rape it took to make that light skin and pretty hair.

A little short bottled-assed man took a liking to my mother. She couldn't stand him. Luella loved him because he was neat, well mannered and she knew the hard working church family he came from. Mom liked them tall dark and handsome with a liking to the sporting life. Gwynedd was a good life with good people, but it was boring. Mom was hungry for excitement—a bigger world. She had been hearing all of this great music on the radio—Billie Holiday was already her favorite. Philly was wide open. She was anxious to be apart of it. No way in the world was she going to settle for a good ole boring ass church man and rock his children for the rest of her life.

Once a year, a train left from Ambler Station to Atlantic City. Baskets were filled with fried chicken and potato salad, homemade beer and wine for the grown folks and sarsaparilla for the kids. Everyone enjoyed the picnic on the train, going from car to car laughing and talking looking out of the window as they went through the countryside. Mom was with her cousin Dorothy and her parents, Dawson and Rosie.

We had to bring our own food because we were not welcomed in the hotels and restaurants.

Besides we didn't have much money anyway. It was supposed to be a fun day. I don't know how it happened, so don't ask me, but it was between Bea and Dora. They got to fussin. One word led to another and then they were in it. They started knocking and slapping each other something terrible. People jumped up to get out of the way and somebody got clucked up side the head with a chicken leg. Dora and Bea were wailing. Bea called Dora a black funky bitch! You know black in those days was a fighting word. Dora tore into Bea and ripped her shirt up. All her titties came falling out for the whole world to see. Dolly gave her his jacket to wear and I think it was Martha who gave her some safety pins to fix herself up a little. I looked at Dorothy and she looked at me and Aunt Rosie looked at both of us. "You betta not move."

It was quiet for the rest of the trip. Atlantic City on the train was a two hour trip. Bea had to wear Dolly's jacket the whole time and it was a hot day too. We walked along the beach, but we didn't set up camp. Coloreds didn't do the beach. Nobody I knew of had a swim suit. I guess some of us didn't know what it was. We walked up and down the boardwalk and took in a few rides. The best part of the trip was just being out with friends and family, enjoying the day together. I had a little money from my days work and brought a little something back for grandmom.

The train left back for Ambler about six in the evening and it was a very quiet ride back home

*after all that carrying on in the morning. When we
pulled into Ambler Station, chicken bones and
paper cups were everywhere. After a while, they
stopped having those trips. Nobody got to go
anywhere. It was getting to be too much. See, we
didn't know how to act even then.*

Going to the city was a big day. For Easter
and maybe Christmas, Aunt Rosie took mom and
Dorothy in town. They went to Ambler Station,
which brought them into Reading Terminal. It was
the first time mom ever saw a flushed toilet and
large sidewalks. They stayed right on Market
Street and kept their eye on the Terminal to keep
from getting lost, never getting to Chestnut Street.
Mom loved and hustle and bustle. She saw the
Earle Theater on the corner of Market Street at
11th. She heard so much about the theater where
Chic Webb was appearing. After shopping and
browsing at either Gimbels or Lit Brothers they
went to the automat for a bite to eat. Aunt Rosie
figured out how to put money in the machine, and
the food came out. They never got food so fast and
it didn't taste bad either. Mom fell in love with the
city. She couldn't get enough of the shops and
excitement. Mom couldn't wait to get away—
break free from Gwynedd.

*People can put shackles on your mouth, but
never let anyone shackle your mind. That is what
most are really after, to control your brain. People*

who aren't able to control or manipulate almost always have a problem and it'll always be your fault. That rings true from the white man to your man. Don't ever forget that.

I heard that warning all of my life and appreciate the dark side of truth that isn't supposed to be addressed. I think about the trends I've seen, the authoritative voice insisting on yes and the rest of us know good and damn well it's a lie. I think about doctrines that are not in the best interest for most and the demand to internalize them anyway and call it right. I know the hunger of wanting to break free.

"I remember I had a bad cold. Grandmom mixed mutton tallow, she called it 'talla' with pure mustard and smeared it on my neck and chest then wrapped me up in a flannel rag. She made a cough syrup from crystal clear rock candy she bought at the drug store with corn liquor and lemon or onion syrup. Then she put an onion under the bed to break the fever. The next day the onion was black and my fever was gone. Every time I sneezed grandmom hollered CATCH EM'!

Asphodeline is a root that smells like strong garlic and onion. A polis was made with the root and pig lard, which served as a salve for all kinds of roots. The old folks called it pneumonia cure and it always required a flannel wrap. Once Aunt Rosie was low sick with a bug. Grandmom rubbed her down with the cure and wrapped her up, and then she heated the flat iron on the stove and put it on top of the wrap like a heating pad. After a few hours, Aunt Rosie coughed up the largest, most disgusting glob of mucus and she felt so much better. The next day she was back to work.

Asphodeline was so strong; it drove you out of the room. You could smell it from here to the William Penn Inn. Some people kept it on all winter, wrapped up in hopes of keeping the flu away. After a while everyone and their house smelled the same. It was terrible. Even after taking a bath there were still remnants in your skin. It didn't clear out until summer. Mom told me that while gazing into a jar of musterole to rub me down and wrap me up.

Spring replenished the land with leaves and roots to clean the body. My mother and Dorothy went into the field to pick Mullen, a broad leaf that looks like a collard green, sassafras and spearmint leaves.

I loved to chew spearmint leaf. It was delicious. It was the closest thing we had for chewing gum. There were all kinds of treats in the field. But you had to know your leaves or you might end up with the shits or a swollen tongue.

Leaf based tonics and teas kept insides clean. Raw sulfur mixed with Black Strap molasses was sucked down to clear the bowels. Grandmom boiled Mullen leaf in a pot of water from the first rain in May to soak her feet and make a warm compress for her knees. Everything was from scratch. Even the drug store made medicine from scratch. Once in a while grandmom had to go to Ambler to Joe Angeny's drug store on Butler Avenue and, of course, mommy tagged along.

I used to love the smell when I first walked in. It was clean and medicinal but pleasant. The wall was lined with dark wood shelving. All of the medicines were white powders in glass jars. The man with the white apron, I didn't know the word pharmacist, got a bowl and peg, and I saw him mix the medicine right in front of us. He ground that stuff until it looked like confection powder and funneled it into a small glass vial. Grandmom bought flax seed, licorice, yeast, hops and coke syrup from the drugstore. She made delicious flax seed tea—cleaned you out real good. For me, the big event was the counter where soda came from a jerk and hand-dipped ice cream. We didn't know anything about box ice cream tasting like the box it came in. It was smooth and creamy and I could taste everything in it, fresh cream and sugar and vanilla.

Nobody hardly ever went to the doctor. Mom didn't waste her money at the drug store buying concoctions either.

"We didn't use none of that stuff except a few aspirins. Grandmom went out in the field and gathered up some roots for me and I was just fine." Stung by a bee —3 leaves peach leaf, pear leaf, and apple leaf; Got a fever —Put an onion under

the bed; stop diarrhea —take down a couple tablespoons of burnt flour; Catch a Cold— a plaster of mustard or asphodeline and mutton tallow or goose grease, rubbed on the chest and bound a with flannel scarf; Indigestion - black pepper and salt; Cut finger— stuff with either cob webs or soot; Bad cough— cook some corn liquor, rock candy and lemon. Dirty windows — kerosene or vinegar and water and newspaper. Arthritis — boil Mullen leaves in a pot of water from the first rain in May.

Pancakes from scratch — Flour – 1 cup, sugar -1 tablespoon, salt -2 pinches, oil -1/4 cup, 2 eggs - milk – 1/3 cup, baking powder – 1 teaspoon.

Some families were completely wiped out from tuberculosis. Back then it was called consumption. Once someone was sick, the entire family was quarantined with a big sign tacked on the door. Neither mom nor her family ever became ill. It was just luck. Many women died in childbirth and sometimes the baby too. It was mostly because the afterbirth wasn't delivered and blood poison set in or they simply bled to death. People didn't know what was wrong with the new mother or how to help her. Mom remembered when Aunt Ella was having some of her children. The bed was padded down with newspaper and clean rags. She told me water was always boiling on the back of everyone's stove. Boiled water was needed to add to a basin to wash hands and to wash the baby. Grandmom went into the cabinet to get the brandy for Aunt Ella to help with those biting labor pains.

They just had to bear with it. They didn't have drugs and for the most part no doctors. Sometimes, Doctor Hawkins, the only black doctor they knew would come by if someone was able to get the word to him in time. Aunt Ella was screaming and hollering upstairs and the midwife was telling her bear down, bear down! When the baby came, it busted her wide open. Women didn't have episiotomies, she was torn open and healed the best way she could. Can you imagine going through that eight, ten or maybe fifteen times?

Just the thought made my behind hurt. It wore women out having so many children and not having medical attention.

You see, they didn't have birth control like they do now. The best hope was maybe a wad of petroleum jelly up there and hope for the best. Women didn't have the option of turning their husband down either. I don't care how tired she was—she had to give it up. It didn't matter if she was tired of having babies. Many women were far along in their pregnancy before they even knew. Just about everyone breast fed, so she had no period. Their only clue was the baby kicking. A few months later, she's gone again. After seven, eight and nine children, she's bound to loose some. It's just the way it was.

Babies often had large navels that stuck out like a thumb, looked like a hernia set way out because the cord wasn't cut properly. Mothers put a quarter on the child to try to set the navel back and bind them with a belly wrap. When babies died, they were put in a shoebox and buried in the field or the woods like a household pet. Where there are houses now were woods and field with many babies underneath. They weren't uncaring or cruel. It was the depth of The Depression. People could hardly eat. No one had money for a funeral. Sometimes the baby was dumped in the outhouse. These were not miscarriages, these were full term babies, big babies; some were still birth. Even if they hat was passed, pennies and maybe a few nickels were the best to be gotten. Very few records were kept of births at that time, and certainly no record of death for an infant child. Many women had a lot of children, and of them half died. Infant mortality was high even for white people.

On December 7, 1941 all hell broke loose. Germany was on one side and Japan on the other. It was the end of the world. The Depression was still on and now this. Everyone had blackout shades. When the sirens went off, the lights went out. If anyone so much as lit a cigarette, they could be put in jail. The entire area went dark. No one looted or committed any crime. They stayed home, obeyed the law and kept still. People were afraid and worn out from years of desperation. Poor grandmom was so afraid she would start praying immediately in the dark and sometimes crawl under the table. She was afraid of the 'bums'.

When the draft went into effect, Ambler Station was turned out and all of the Italian ladies were there bidding their husbands, brothers, and sons farewell. They were some praying women too. Mom said they held their rosaries, spoke their native Italian and put down a moving prayer for everybody who was there.

The priest from Saint Mary's and Reverend Holden had service on the platform. You never saw so much praying in all your life. People were kissing each other, kissing the ground. People who hadn't spoke in years spoke that day. All of my Penllyn cousins and Ambler boys were gone. But I tell ya, that's when the good times started. Norristown, Philly, D.C., it was jumpin!

Jazz finally reached Gwynedd and was a companion for my mother. Duke, Ella, Count, Lady Day, Sassy, Goodman and Nat King Cole were her touchstones. There were songs that reflected the era known as war songs; *G.I. Jive* and *Inflation Blues*. She sang along with the radio emulating Billie Holiday. Singing was her passion. Her outlet wasn't available until years later, but she was free for three minutes. She spent some Saturday afternoons at the movies to see her favorite stars and developed a taste for classical music.

Mom was seventeen and stayed home from school one day to take care of Momma Lou. She wasn't feeling very well and wanted to go upstairs to lie down. Mom played the piano until grandmom asked her to stop all the noise. She decided to go into the kitchen and get some ironing done. It was the only thing she could do quietly. Her cousin Dorothy had gone to school that day and was home by about 3:30 pm. She immediately felt a strange force in the house but couldn't put her finger on it. She asked mom "Don't you feel that? Something is wrong."

Mom had no idea what she was talking about, but as an old school note, Dorothy was born with a veil on her face. Legend has it that babies born with veils, a thin membrane covering their face, are supposed to have premonitions that escape the rest of us. Neither of them ever thought to go upstairs.

"Where's grandmom?" Dorothy asked.

"Upstairs sleep. She said she didn't feel well." Mom replied, never once looking up from her ironing.

Aunt Nina came by everyday to check on her aging mother-in-law she always called Missus Williams. She went up the stairs and looked over into the middle bedroom and saw that Missus Williams was gone.

Luella Williams peacefully died in her sleep Monday, May 25, 1942 in the same room where

she had given birth to my grandmother Homzell—
the same room Homzell gave birth to my mother,
Hazel. Momma Lou never had an education, but a
belly full of wisdom. She was guided by her faith
and some of old beliefs of the time. Her wisdom
guided my mother—even in confusion–through
her battles to listen to her conscious for guidance.
She told her granddaughter that if she was ever in
doubt to do nothing—hold a quarter up to a quarter
moon for good luck—never look to people, but to
the Almighty for guidance and comfort.

The undertaker, Bob Smith, embalmed her
in the room. Her body was placed in a casket in the
same room. Her funeral was Thursday, the day off
for domestic workers.

Old folks put the fear of dead people in
children early. Mom and Dorothy had three
sleepless nights while their grandmother laid cold
down the hall. Her funeral was May 28, at
Bethlehem Baptist Church and she was buried in
Rose Valley cemetery next to her husband
Shadrack.

Uncle Dawson and Aunt Rosie moved to
rent a house in Ambler. Aunt Nina and Uncle Lush
separated for a while. Uncle George had eight
children. Aunt Bert didn't want much bother. My
grandmother, Homzell was sleeping in. Mommy's
fathers' people, the Johnson's, all had a house full
of children. Dorothy went with her mother and
father and later married.

I didn't know what to do. I was seventeen

and still a kid. People had their own problems. I remembered what my grandmother told me. I left Gwynedd and went to Ambler with Aunt Rosie, and then I went to Chestnut Hill looking for a sleep in job.

Three weeks after the death of her grandmother, mom graduated from Ambler High School. Her future was uncertain at best, but little did she know there were harsh and beautiful times that lie ahead.

After Luella's death in May, 1942, Aunt Rosie and Uncle Dawson moved to South Ambler in September of the same year. Meanwhile Joe, my mother's first cousin, married Verlie Free in 1938 and resided in Bryn Mawr and later moved into the house in Gwynedd and installed indoor plumbing in 1943. Mommy tucked in with them for a while.

The farm was now a barren field. The livestock either died off or was sold. Mom was about eighteen and trying to get on her feet. Cousin Joe didn't want her there because she didn't have a job and was eating on his biscuit. He was working at SmithKline and French in West Point PA. He started to raise a little hell about it much to cousin Verlie's dismay. Aunt Rosie had a few choice words for Joe and invited mom to go to Ambler and live with her and Dawson. She packed up and moved in with her aunt and uncle for a while, but she wasn't any better off. She had to share Dorothy's bed who did not like it at all and let her know it, and to think they grew up sharing everything as children. Dorothy would do things like snatch all the covers off mom reminding her it was Dorothy's father, not hers who provided. They argued and fought. It didn't matter who won or lost, tension ultimately beat them both. Mom's resentment became her source of strength. She had days work here and there for a while, nothing steady. On hard luck days she didn't have work, but she still had to eat.

Aunt Rosie started signifying about how high food was and made every guilt ridden bite almost indigestible. It's hard to live in a place where you're not wanted. Having no one to turn to is worse than being poor, and when you're both poor and alone, it's the darkest valley to walk.

Aunt Rosie and Uncle Dawson bought an old Bocce house owned by the Son's of Italy on Wissahickon Avenue in South Ambler.

The Village of Wissahickon was and old mill town since the Civil War. The village was renamed Ambler in 1869 after a Quaker woman. Mattison, co-founder of Keasby and Mattison Asbestos Mill, had modest homes built by Italian masons to house employees working in the mill. By the forties, these houses were usable but, some were showing signs of decay. The Italians owned the mill houses and rented them to blacks.

Aunt Rosie took in roomers. Mommy's Cousin Jean, moved in with her husband Walter and his mother Miss Viola. Thelma Tate and her husband Melvin were just up from Westmoreland also squeezed in. All these people were living in the house with one bathroom. There was drama every day.

Ambler ain't nothing but Westmoreland County. There were several families; the Deans, the Ducketts, the Mahoney's and many more. Everybody intermarried into these different families and the kids all come out cousins. It was like little Harlem. You never heard so much mess in

*all your life. People were all up in everybody's
business, but if somebody was known to carry
tales, they were the first to get a reputation for
being gossipy. Even after the people died, people
still talked about all the shit they did. The men
worked at the mill and the women either worked
for the white folks or they were home all day. The
mill had several shifts. When the five o'clock
whistle blew, the alley was hot with outside lovers
running home before the husband got home. It
looked like everybody was going with each others'
husband or wife and they were supposed to be
friends. You know talk got back. It was typical
small town mess.*

The Italians had their side of town and the
blacks had the other side and everyone got along
just fine. The south side was considered a small
ghetto because it was hot with action. Complete
with the infamous asbestos mountain, South
Ambler was notorious for drinking, gambling and
butt chasing every Saturday night in the alleys.
There was the Up Alley and the Down Alley also
known as Signors Alley, the owner of the rented
homes. Respectable people sneaked in, had some
fun, wiped their mouth and talked down the people
who lived there.

The Italian ladies were good to anyone
having a hard time. They grew the prettiest
tomatoes in the backyard and cooked their ass off.
It was in Ambler where mom got her first real taste
of Italian food. Tenor arias were as much a part of

the morning as the dew when husbands tended to the garden and wives prepared pasta, basil tomato sauce, and delicious fresh baked bread. She noticed that they always seemed to wear black and stayed very close to home. Most were not allowed on the avenue and didn't dare cross the tracks after six pm. Their homemade dishes and preserves helped get many of the new arrivals through cold harsh winters. Even the men who owned the houses would help. If someone was having a hard time finding work or paying the rent, they would let them slide. The Italians provided housing, entertainment and loans for everyone and got plenty rich from the population.

Butler Avenue is the main street where people did Saturday morning shopping. The small town thoroughfare was lined with dress shops, grocery stores and the Ambler Movies. Grown folks got the latest gossip and children saw their friends.

Caviler's night club on Butler Avenue was mom's first peek at the world of Saturday night, the night her grandmother furiously denounced. She was escorted by her curious Ambler friends for a taste of forbidden escapades. The nickelodeon kept toes tapping. Special nights featured live music by none other than organist Henry *Oh Yea*! Carter. He was a smack in the ass for everyone. Ladies sat at tables, never the bar having potential beaus buy them drinks. Soldier boys told their ugly stories about the war—lice and body parts—how

racism disappeared in those dirty foxes holes.
Some had to smell each others' stench and wear
their own waste. Mom heard John Willie Gaskins
from Ambler talk about black men throwing white
bigots overboard accidentally—or shot—by enemy
fire. Men returning from war were in what was
called the 52/20 club; they got a check for twenty
dollars for a year and proudly wore the ruptured
duck pin. G.I.'s were prime pickings for any young
girl looking for a man with a reliable check.

Jimmy had the Greek was the owner of a
club called Ambler Palace at the corner of Butler
and Maple. John Willie earned the Purple Heart in
WWII and was glad to be home. To celebrate, he
went to the Ambler Palace for a drink with a few
of his buddies, but he had to integrate it first. He
and his friends were directed to go through the
back door. John Willie had a democratic fit.

"I got my ass blown off, for you! Been to
hell and back a couple of times and I can't come
home to have a drink and sit where I want?!" he
said. After he beautifully cussed out the owner,
John Willie brought his other black buddies in the
front door and demanded them to sit wherever they
wanted and enjoy their drinks. People black and
white sat where they wanted ever since that day.
John Willie was a founding member of Daniel
Dowling post number 769. He wore a white cap
for the ninth district of Sergeant Arms along with
Walter Kelly and Earl Henry who was nicknamed
Chappy. John Willie started the American Legion

in Ambler. He knew how to command order and attention better than the police and took absolutely no shit off of anybody, black or white.

He directed the Memorial Day ceremony every year at Rose Valley Cemetery. He was in his heaven directing traffic at the funerals. With John Willie leading the procession, he made sure the white folks waited. He subversively rejoiced when he had the power over white folks making them wait longer than necessary giving us right of way first.

"Let'em wait, they ain't going nowhere." he'd say.

Momma didn't like most of the men who passed through her life. Now matter how broke a man was, he was still king. Men folks were something. They ruled the world and tried to rule women. Some didn't respect women because they were afraid of being henpecked. They didn't know the difference between being a male and being a man. Some kept their women broke and pregnant while they had as many women as they wanted to. Women usually had no where to go, a house full of children and no living wage job. Many died from too many pregnancies, malnutrition and abuse. Others stood up to him; strong and raw because they had to be.

Miss Martha was nobody to fool with. She lived in South Ambler and was as rough as any man. I remember walking up Locust Street on my way to Butler Avenue. Some man was giving her a hard time about something. All I could hear was Miss Martha cussing this man out. When she got hot, it was a stage show;

I'm thirty six across my breast; I don't fear nothing but Gawd and death; I don't own no house, but I paid my rent; and I don't owe a mother fucka a goddamn cent. **Now beat me**! *It was enough for me to stay clear. That's how they were sometimes. It was too rugged for me. People were going with people they had no business, staying drunk, and kept a lot of shit going all the time. Two women on Butler Avenue got to fightin over the same man. They both had kids for him. One was the wife and the other was the outside woman. People would come running all through the neighborhood yelling. They fightin! Come on, they fightin yall! It was something. Mops and buckets dropped and they went flying up on the avenue. They beat the shit out of each other. It was outright funky. The crowd sided with the wife, but it was the other woman who was kicking ass.*

It all got to be just too much for mom. It wasn't enough to just mind your own business. People have a way of pulling you into something you had nothing to do with, and you wake up wondering how in the devil you got in this mess and worse how to get out of it.

I had to get away from that mess. Every time I turned around, somebody was getting cussed out, beat up or having a baby by the wrong person. I did just what grandmom told me to do. I got a sleep-in job in Chestnut Hill on Seminole Avenue. He was a lawyer. Every morning I had to make that three minute egg with a slice of toast and a cup of coffee. I got so sick of that three minute egg, sick of the toast, sick of them but what am I going to do? Talk about boredom.

This family took summer vacations in Stone Harbor. Mommy's job of course was to watch the children and keep house while the grown folks were out for enjoyment. They were the boring days of summer with nothing to do but watch the ladies sit around and talk about kids, recipes, and plants all day long. Some children were allowed to get away with a lot more than would have ever been permitted in her childhood. They were allowed to have tantrums, talk back and throw things in a fit of anger. They were allowed to pout and would sometimes end up having their way.

You know the old folks I came from wouldn't have it. They didn't need or have experts and children didn't have their way, point blank. There was never an argument that I knew of between parent and child. If there was I would've heard about it. I had to watch these little shits have a fit until they got their way.

She longed for the delightful sounds of Louis Armstrong, Duke Ellington and Billie Holiday, but settled for the Andrew Sisters, Bing Crosby and Kate Smith. Her days off were worse than the days she worked. There wasn't anything for her to do. She didn't know anyone and most places weren't very pleased to have coloreds in their establishments. She ended up spending all day at the movies.

It was a different story with the men. After the women and children were asleep, the men got together and went to Atlantic City where the black folks were partying on Kentucky Avenue. They went to the clubs, got a little bit, wiped their mouth and came home to their pretentious, boring families. They wouldn't dare let their family and friends know they took a liking to dark meat. They went about their day as if the help was nobody, therefore no need to consider anything. That's how mom knew their secrets. They whispered in corners, but it didn't help because their behavior revealed their mentality.

Everyone who did days' work or sleep-in had off every Thursday and every other Sunday. Thursdays were known as pot slingers day or sud-busters day. I loved to go into town to the movies on Thursdays. Movie houses were closed on Sunday, so sometimes I went to Ambler to visit family and friends. I had a chance to catch up on what was going on. I even went to visit Uncle Dossy and Aunt Rosie. Old evil-assed Uncle Dossy looked at me with a suspicious eye.

"I guess you living down there in South Philly huh?" He said it in such a way mom wasn't sure if it was a statement or a question. Uncle Dossy really pissed her off. She cussed him out and sent him to hell in her heart, but sheepishly answered,

"No, I'm with a family in Chestnut Hill." He was always trying to cut her down. He was sure no good could come to her fooling around in the city by herself. She either had to end up with a house full of children fathered by everybody or become a whorish drunk, or both.

"I hope you ain't singing in them bars and stuff. Gal you need to get yourself right. Don't be like your ole mother!" Aunt Rosie said from across the room.

Mommy didn't dare sass back, but didn't bother with them either. She was doing alright for herself and thanks to his nasty ass; she was stronger because now she understood what ignorance sounded like. She strolled over to see her old friend Emma who told her about the tuberculosis problem that had taken many families out. Mommy's friend Mignonette Smith died at the age of 18 in the fall of 1943 and her sister Mary Jane died at 15; her father, mother and brother were all gone from TB. One brother survived but had been taken to Hamburg PA. They lived on Orange Avenue. The whole town was almost wiped out. Survivors fled to the mountains. Asbestosis and cirrhosis took out the rest of the population. Ambler was clearing out fast.

Mom kept looking in the paper and got a better job. She found one at the Widener Estate farm on Bethlehem Pike and Haws Lane. The pay was much better, twenty five dollars a week plus meals. Over time, she got to know some of the other house ladies and they shared stories. They kept close to one another for support and learning. They learned games and gimmicks played by some of their employers and got together when they could to talk over the backyard fence while hanging the wash. It seemed some poorer white women were often the worst ones to work for— using their whiteness as a weapon expecting their ass to be kissed and Miss colored lady to be thankful for any stale crumbs that were thrown with contempt. They tried the dumbest tricks like leaving money around the house to see who would steal. How else could one explain a twenty dollar bill under the sofa cushion? Another twenty somehow slipped into the radiator column. Or get this one—a signed blank check under the bed. Miss Lily was forever 'misplacing' things around the house. Seems to me if it was so valuable, it would be put away for safe keeping. After all, they had special shelving for liquor— kept that wine under lock and key. Many colored women worked with the air thick with accusing eyes and presumption of guilt. Momma said white people have heard all their life that coloreds steal and lie. To argue back would make Miss Lily a liar or accusing her of being one. Add some intelligence, which could be as simple as the truth, now she's uppity. Cullards were supposed to be stupid too.

That was the hardest thing about sleeping in. You washed and ironed, cooked and cleaned for the family all day. It's not like they gave you anything, but some thought they did. There were those who were alright, but there were nasty bitches in the mix. I remember one young girl who worked in Chestnut Hill near me. That lady harassed that poor girl to death. She accused that girl of lying, stealing; calling her stupid and one time I heard from the other housekeepers she smacked the girl. It was rumored that the woman's husband got a little bit or tried to. To look at the couple, you'd never know. They were typical white upper class folks. After a while, I didn't see the girl anymore. I was told she left, but got a good one in before she did. Her fear and frustration turned to anger. She couldn't decide whether to pee in the tea or spit in it. Then her time came. Yea, she served the tea alright. The last I heard she married a soldier man and moved into Philly.

The employment agency had plenty of day work. They gave the address and off you went. The lady told her maid of the day what she wanted done and sometimes had to show her how to use new appliances like vacuum cleaners, washing machines, pop-up toasters and paid her at the end of the day. I remember one cleaning lady got a knock on the door. It was the police saying the lady she worked for that day had some things missing. I think it was jewelry. The cleaning woman really had no idea what was going on because she knew she hadn't taken anything. The fact that the law knocked on her door was traumatizing enough. Even when you tell the truth, you're lying. As it turned out the woman happened to find what she thought she lost, the policeman let the cleaning lady know she was off the hook with no apology, no explanation, nothing. It was big talk among the housemaids the next day. Something else to watch out for.

This is what some black women went through to earn an honest living, threats silently looming over their head. Wealthier families were a little easier. The woman I worked for liked to feed her dog lamb loin chops. I had to prepare the luscious chops for the dog, but I was supposed to eat leftovers. Many afternoons the dog ate the leftovers and I ate the lamb chops.

When the war began, jobs became available for coloreds and women. People were pulled off the street to start training immediately. For the first time, Miss Lily had to do her own washing and ironing and cooking. Newspapers were filled with ads, cries and pleas for maids and cleaning ladies. Colored women quit doing days work and went into the factories for their first real pay envelope.

Philly was a factory town; Queen Casuals, Stetson Hats, Botany 500. Bayuk Cigar Factory was at 8th and Columbia and just across the river was Campbell's Soup where mom worked for a little while picking bad tomatoes off the conveyor belt. Weekly pay was a cash envelope.

The city had its racial lines. White women were generally from Logan and Olney —the northeast was new and some parts were yet to be built. Black folks mostly lived in North and South Philly. Needless to say the white women got the better jobs and made life hell for the black women. The floor lady was always white and gave the worst job to the black women. Shit was purposely shoved her way and if she fought back she was easily fired. If the black woman had a job that the white woman wanted, the floor lady could easily get rid of her. If she was late getting back from break, she was ratted out by the white co-worker. Nothing was said when the white woman was late. Sometimes, even if they just didn't want to look at a black face, anything could be said: the black lady was working too slowly; her machine keeps breaking down; she's not doing the work right; something, anything to get rid of her. All of this was done behind her back. They stuck it to the black women because they could. Mom worked in one of these factories alongside a woman whose whiteness was supreme.

Colored women had a hard time trying to keep a job, especially if they were dark skinned. The light ones had it a little better. Black woman who passed for white had it the best. They played white folks at their own game, but it was a lot of strife between them and dark skinned women.

I loved the fact that a few of us who could pass were working there in their face. We laughed everyday knowing they're not as bright as they thought they were. They were talking about black people not knowing they were talking to one.

There were no Jim Crow laws in the north but there was segregation. Even in a little nothing place like a diner, coloreds weren't denied service, but left a lot to be desired. Pork yak was mommy's weekly treat at a Chinese restaurant in North Philly. But after eating the meal, she kept getting sick and couldn't figure out why. Later the place was busted. The newspaper stated that the owner had indeed used cat meat to make his food, but it was okay because he only served it to the niggers. The fur in his trash was the clue.

My father, Bennie arrived in Philadelphia in 1947 from Durham, North Carolina. He was tall, red and slender with sandy brown hair—a plum nellie happy to be out of Jim Crow south and in the land where he thought opportunity and promise were abundant. He really wanted to go into the service but by the time he was eighteen, World War II was over. He began with odd jobs setting up bowling pins and washing dishes at any restaurant.

While working at Duphers Hospital in Jarretown, a co-worker invited him to hang out for a bit in Ambler. Mom went to Ambler too. Her paternal grandfather was a Pullman chef on the Reading line, then worked the kitchen at Cavalier's on Butler Avenue where she was welcome to eat and drink as much as her belly could hold. Through mutual friends, my parents, Hazel and

Bennie met at club Cavaliers. Billie Holiday's *You go to my Head* was their first dance. She took a liking to him because he was quiet and reserved. She forgot about still waters running deep. All she knew was that he was different from the Ambler and Norristown men who were either rowdy or country and backward. She wanted someone who wasn't from the area, someone who wasn't sleeping around with everybody or raising hell. But he was lost too. They clung to each other. They had nobody else.

Soon mom left her sleep-in job to be with her young love. They were married in Elkton, Maryland, 1948. Plenty of days work was available in North Philly especially in all white Strawberry Mansion. They rented a room on Oxford Street—the second floor back. Kitchen privileges were extra. A small lock on the rotary phone kept people from running up the phone bill. Anyone could receive calls, but nobody except the owner could make them. They ate out every night at either Father Divine or any greasy spoon they could afford. George Baker, a.k.a. Father Divine, developed a Peace Mission during the 1930s, giving relief to people hard on their luck. He bought hotels and stores in Atlantic City, New York City and Philadelphia. Fifteen cents bought a hot home cooked meal.

Dad did day work at the docks unloading whatever came in. One day he unloaded a ship full of bananas and that's what they had for dinner that night, bananas. Mom worked at a factory on Callowhill Street inspecting bottle tops. During tomato season, she did piece work at Campbell's Soup inspecting tomatoes on the conveyor belt and did days work in between. It put her in mind of the old days when she helped her grandmother can all kinds of vegetables for the winter. She had it down and was making good money. Then she was promoted to noodles. The tomato department only lasted as long as the season, noodles was steadier work. She washed and boiled noodles all day. One week she made eighty dollars! They paid their rent, put some away and ate at Father Divine's communion table, twenty five cents, and took in a movie. People got dressed up to go to the movies. In their Sunday best they went to see movies like *Gaslight, Shadow of a Doubt, Johnny Belinda* and *Mildred Pierce.*

In 1949 with the advice from the insurance man, mom got in touch with a nice family who rented the entire third floor to them at 1339 north 21st street near Master. They were able to move from the second floor back into their first apartment in the private home of Mister and Missus Cook. They had comfort, safety and stability they needed in a new, strange often frightening city. The second and third floors were sometimes the only income some families had and the only place most people could afford to live. When the rent was too high or money was short, people moved out in the middle of the night. It was called 'carrying the stick'. Mom and dad carried many sticks before coming to the Cooks. Mister Cook was a stately Indian brown man, tall and slender and had his own junkman business. He had lost his sight to Glaucoma. His wife Nettie, light skinned and petite, did house work. To mom, Missus Cook looked a lot like Aunt Nina. He was a frugal man who furnished his house, bought his home and saved good money hauling junk. They were fifty something middle class coloreds and welcomed mom and dad into their humble home. They admired the young country couple and took them on as their own children. Mister Cook schooled them both about they ways of the city. He told them to watch out for the Pigeon Drop— people looking for you to put up money in *good faith* to share in money they say they found. Anybody asking for money to secure a good deal was a thief. Missus Cook told mom to watch her drink when she went out. Mickey Finn was the name for the knock out drug used to put in a woman's drink. Either take your drink with you or get a fresh one—and watch the bartender too. You never know who he's in cahoots with. Mister and Missus Cook became Aunt Nettie and Uncle Will to mom. At last she felt like she had a family again.

Dad finally got a full time job. He was an official janitor at Wyeth Labs at 12th and Washington Avenue with a steady income of fifty dollars a week. As profits increased for the company so did wages making life a little easier for poor people. One salary was enough to keep a small family comfortable. With a steady job and a nice apartment they were starting to prosper. Christmas was just around the corner. Mom marched up on Ridge Avenue and bought a little tree, just enough for the two of them. She stopped at a local retail store to buy trimmings and electric lights for their first Christmas in their first apartment. They sat up all night just looking at that tree, ate regular home cooked meals and opened a savings account at First National Bank and looked forward to doing Saturday grocery shopping.

Market Street was lined with furniture stores like 606 Market Street, Bailey's Furniture, Frank and Cedars department Store, Mary Jane Dress Shop and various haberdasheries and millineries.

Mom and dad enjoyed their little palace and passed the time away with music. Dad strummed his guitar he bought from the pawn shop. After dinner, he and mom sang. Together they improvised their own arrangements to the standards of the day like *Stardust* and *Body and Soul*. They sang a lot of gospel: *In the Garden, Blessed Assurance, God Is Real.* Uncle Will and Aunt Nettie enjoyed their evening listening to the two of them.

Mommy, Hazel Johnson newly arrived in Philly, 1946

Things were getting a little better, but their struggle was far from over. Barely on their feet, they had to contend with dad's brothers and sisters. They came north to the only people they knew, their brother and sister-in-law. They had no jobs, no prospects, and no interest. They ate right into the feeble cookie jar that took so long to build. Mom and dad had to pay Uncle Will extra rent for the room down the hall to house brother Buttercup and help the sister with every baby she had.

After a year at Wyeth and a pay raise or two, they bought a television. It was a large, tall consol with a screen about the size of a postage stamp. They had television parties to watch the fights. It was impressive when people saw the blue light shining through the window. Then they got a black rotary telephone. It was a party line. That meant at any time mom picked up the phone someone could already be on the line. If she wanted to use the phone she had to wait for them to get off.

The forties and fifties were good times and bad. Momma took me to WWII. That's right she took me there to the condition of humanity during the war. We were going through a lot. Germany was on one side and Japan on the other and the unrelenting apartheid right here in the good ole U.S. of A. We were still suffering from the ravages of The Depression and most people didn't have antibiotics. Going to school and taking a bath for many was still far from commonplace. The pot was

on a slow boil on both sides of the Mason Dixon
Line. In the north, some blacks were abused with
high rent, living packed on top of each other and
low pay if they had a job at all. They were cheated
in stores, endured a Jim Crow military, red lined
out of neighborhoods and suffered daily contempt
from whites, unless they opted for arrest, an ass
whipping or death instead. Blacks were at the
mercy of racist cops and thieves who presented
themselves as lenders. A contagious spirit of
determination and pride was bubbling. Mom
wasn't politically inclined, but she felt the fever.
She witnessed these goings on and how people
acted and reacted to current events of the time. It's
sort of like now. The air is irritated with evil, but
no matter how loud the scream, there's no sound.

Billie Holiday's anthem of *Strange Fruit*
shamed America to look its lie. Music and theater
possessed a power the dominant culture couldn't
control—or understand. Jazz was a spiritual tonic
that soothed the soul and helped it endure for a
better day.

Ridge Avenue was enjoyable. Pleasant
evenings were spent walking up and down licking
ice cream cones, window shopping, meeting and
greeting neighbors. The gas man came around
every evening to light the gas lamps that lined the
streets while the hot summer breeze invited
everyone outside. People were going to the movies
and clubs dressed in their finest. North Philly was
peaceful. Doors and windows were left open at

night. Times were hard, but doable because people were practical. Five or six dollars bought everything needed. A shot of liquor cost thirty five cents. Cigarettes were bought by the pack for a quarter, or one at a time, loosies. Gasoline was about thirty five cents a gallon. Clubs and eateries bustled—A Bucket of Blood, Piggy's, Checker Club, The Cotton Club and The Carioca Club. Gentlemen tipped their hat when a lady passed and ladies never, not even the loose ones, went in the front entrance. They went in the side door that was specifically for ladies and sat at a table. It was considered crude for woman walk in the front door and sit at the bar, with her foot on the rail. Live music entertained the street and pulled people in to listen. There was no cover charge and no minimum requirement. People came in to sing and others came to play. Customers were allowed to dance and sometimes played their axe. That was freedom.

Weekly earnings for some were as high as fifty dollars at one of the many factories and the going rate for days work was about four dollars to six dollars a day. Rent was about forty dollars a month. A lot could be done with a little. Butter was about twenty five cents a pound and coffee was thirty five cents and there was no such thing as car insurance. A driver's license wasn't required until Roosevelt came in office. The insurance man made neighborhood rounds to collect for life insurance.

Mom had the sweetest third floor apartment and she could look right over to Eastern State

Penitentiary and see the guard on patrol. Slick
Willie was in there when they could catch him.
Every time a prisoner escaped the sirens went off.
Porch roofs gave escapees easy access to homes
near the prison. The pounding of feet could be
heard running the roof top deep in the night. She
petted and pampered her apartment with doilies,
plastic flowers and knick knacks from the five and
dime store and sometimes nice things she got from
doing days work. She kept everything polished and
puffed up all the time with so much pride. It was
the first time she really felt like she was home
since her grandmother's death. It didn't make a
difference to the mice. She heard them scratching
through the house all night long. One night she
said she caught nine mice. She plopped them in the
toilet from the trap and slammed the lid flushing
all night sometimes, trying to keep the body count
under control. The roof was right outside her third
floor window where the garbage cans were stored
and an open invitation for bats. When they flew in,
mom flew out. Uncle Will gave her collapsible
screens for the windows.

   People believed in and supported one
another to get through the hard times. Parents,
church and teachers had control over children.
Neighbors were extended family and took care of
each other's children with love and reprimand the
same as they had for their own. If someone had
little or nothing to eat, pots of beans and bread
were shared to anyone in need. Children's clothes

were passed around. Word of a job was spread quickly. Sitting on the marble stoop was the only way to catch a warm summer breeze. It brought everyone out for the newest gossip and kitchen tables were hot with Poker and Pinochle. Every night was like a family reunion.

Mom finally got to see her idol Miss Billie Holiday who appeared at the Blue Note located at 16th and Ridge, and again at the Earle Theater on Market Street. The Earle became her favorite spot to see all of the idols of the time. It was a big night to see a show. She said it was like Radio City Music Hall in New York. The theater started with a movie, and then the show began.

Billie Holiday was with Count Basie. I was all week getting ready. People dressed up to go out anywhere. Dress, grace and poise were pride. There was a Miss Laura or a Miss Eva in every neighborhood who did hair or sew up clothes. Even the no good Saturday night men knew how to treat the ladies. Ladies and Gentlemen lived up to the title, at least on the surface and it made for a beautiful evening of entertainment.

Movies and theaters were all over town and was where many celebrities got their start. The Royal Theater at 16th and South featured the Parisian Theater Kiddy Hour sponsored by Horn and Hardhart. Momma saw Etta James get her start. Pearl Bailey lived in North Philly starting her career at the Pearl Theater. Here and there, mom said she sang at little clubs up and down just for fun.

By the early 1950s, my mother took
fellowship at Tenth Memorial Baptist Church;
Reverend Dixon was pastor. She loved church—
loved hearing the gospel. She said it generated
visceral strength no man can kill. But she didn't
know what to make of some preachers, cultists and
evangelists who for the most part wanted to
separate people from their money.

*I saw a preacher hooping and hollering the
gospel, and then he'd shout out "Read!" Then I
heard a man read a passage from the bible, then
the preacher started going on again. I never saw
nothing like that before in my life.*

*Prophet Cherry was at 22nd Street near
Susquehanna. Mother and Father Dabney's
Garden of Prayer was down the street. Sister
Rosetta Thorpe was out there with her tambourine
and guitar. I really liked her too. I caught her every
time I could. But there were other people out there
who had all kinds of tonics and potions to cure and
heal. One was called Uncle Tom's Black Pussyfoot
Oil. It was supposed to cure everything. Another
one was Hatacol. The ad said last call for Hatacol!
People sold it on the avenue and door to door.*

*Most of those preachers put down a good
prayer. Sweet Daddy Grace, Father Divine and
Elder Micheaux were gonna take everybody to the
Promised Land. Some of them told people they
didn't need money. All they needed was the Lord.
They were supposed to give up everything they had*

to be blessed.

Among the good people as usual were those out to scam. They would make a turban out of a white pillow case and a toga-like outfit from a sheet. Many wore sandals and blackened their feet with soot, then sat on an orange crate with a tambourine, start praying, singing and preaching with a bottle of snake oil. The oil could have been anything from olive oil or pig lard to hair grease, who knows? A real snake or maybe just a worm was placed in the bottle for shock effect. It was enough to start people talking. They didn't know what to think.

I just watched 'em. I never saw such a sight all up and down. I was used to preaching in church, not the street corner. It was mesmerizing. Some characters had potions with nails in the bottom of a bottle. That was supposed to represent the devil coming out. Healing tents, traveling revivals were all over. Jack Coe and Thea Jones were at the Met. They were good. I loved to hear them preach. I just couldn't get with the ones who were dressing better than me and looking for my money. Like anything else, there was the righteous mixed up with the shysters who were preaching and begging. I never heard so many lies in all my life. People went for it because it was still a desperate time. It was easy to sell hopes and dreams. Disenchanted populations are always vulnerable to anything that feels good. People took the shoes off of their feet, draws off their ass and the coat off their back. They took money they should have used to buy food and gave it to the mission in hopes of being cured and blessed. It was something. Grocery stores, night clubs and preachers were all mixed up together. A revival shouting could be on one side of the street and a club was jumping on the other side while people were hustling money in the name of the Lord. I think some of the shysters thought God told them to live in splendor. There were some who came out on the street looking like a pimp. Their clothes looked like draperies someone ran up on the machine. Some had silk Mohair, fine threads with konked hair. You could see your face in his shoes. I used to take Uncle Will to the healing tent. He wanted to see again. The preacher told Mister Cook to throw away his glasses because he was going to be healed. Uncle Will threw his glasses and preacher man put that Uncle Toms Black Pussyfoot Oil on his eyes and the next day—he had to buy another pair of dark glasses. When Uncle Will died he was still blind. A woman claimed she had cancer and was desperate for healing. He took a big handful of oil and rubbed his hands all over her body, maybe just feeling her up, probably had a whole hand full of ass and tits. That's how some of them were. Now Father Divine really did help people. He fed a whole lot of poor people including your father and me. He married a pretty Canadian girl who was Mother Divine. He had another place at Broad and Christian. People lined up out the door to get a good meal and hear some good preaching. People picked up soda bottles and redeemed the nickels to eat at Father Divine's.

Roosevelt's New Deal meant that people had to file income tax and some were beginning to receive Social Security checks. Thanks to the industrial explosion and war profits, we entered an era of conveniences like frozen foods and range top stoves. The first ones were coal oil stoves with wick burners. The gas was turned on manually and the wick ignited with a lit match. Fridgidaire put the ice man out of business. Toasters, blenders and vacuums were coming out. Everything that was needed to make doing days work just a little easier—coloreds certainly couldn't afford them.

Federal dollars promoted new highways and single family suburban homes for white folks and public housing for coloreds through the 1950s. Poor folks were packed tight into nice family apartments. Only married couples could move in. People were not hanging on the corner and stirring up trouble. The fronts were swept up and children were tended to. Men went to work, partied on Saturday night and went to church every Sunday.

Dad was promoted from janitor into manufacturing. They bought a car for eight hundred dollars! A 1957 Chevy Bellaire and had no license to drive. Mom had learned how to drive stick shift years ago on the tractor, but had to learn how to drive an automatic. It wasn't common for women, especially black women to know how to drive. Their new Chevy had a special feature called the High Drive. That meant it could be driven as a stick or as an automatic. Their next mission was to move off that third floor apartment and buy their first home.

Dad went to jam sessions all over town. There wasn't any pay, but it was chance to be heard. He was later hired by house bands as a side man. One evening could bring as much as five dollars. It was easy to make an honest hustle before mercantile license and miscellaneous taxes took it away. In addition to steady work, now they had some side money. Mom kept working and saving as much as she could.

Mom's first trip down south was in 1953. She had never been any further south than Westmoreland County, Virginia. She was so excited anticipating meeting her new in-laws. She went to her hair dresser, Bailey's, at 15th and Lombard for a press and curl. There were no perms in those days. Then she went in town on Market Street, when Market Street was Market Street, to buy nice little summer outfits, cute little sandals and told everyone of her impending trip. You might have thought she was going to Paris. They took an un-air-conditioned Trailway bus in mid-July. There was no Interstate 95 either, Route 1 was the only way and that meant going through every single whistle stop town all the way. They had to change buses in Washington D.C. Jim Crow said they had to change their seat too. Mom, knowing she was cute with her broomstick skirt and raggedy assed suitcase, and not knowing any better walked into the white folk's bathroom during the layover and dad had to run after her. No one said anything, but she was given hard, cold, hateful looks....for a long time. In the back of the bus, they continued on their long, hot, ride to Durham, North Carolina. The further down they went, the hotter it was with opened windows, dust and bugs flying and momma still thought she had it going on.

She admired the beautiful collard greens in the field. She had never seen them so green and so big. She stood corrected when dad told her it was tobacco. Meanwhile word in Durham spread that Benny Lee was coming to town and bringing his bride from Philadelphia. They came across the hills and valleys and up off the fields to meet Benny Lee's wife. When mom and dad finally got there, they had to get a cab to his mother's house. It cost twenty-five cents.

Arriving at the house, mom was shocked. She never saw such a sight in her life. A ragged shanty house supported by cinder blocks on a dirt road. Hotels were not an option. Restaurants weren't either. A big black woman stood on the front porch hollering 'Lawd a mussy! The chillun

done come home!' There were her in-laws; cousin
Pokey, Uncle Jimmy, Buttercup, Gaynell, Leroy
and Wesley. Hot as hell and her new do was done.
Red clay dirt and stones from the dusty roads got
all up under her feet, chewed up the soles of her
sandals and chipped the paint off of her toenails.
Just when she thought it couldn't get worse, a
passing car ignited a dust storm. It took fifteen
minutes for the dust to settle, just in time for
another car. It wasn't any better in the little
clapboard house. The windows were open and dust
and flies were everywhere. It was one of those run-
through houses, where you can run through the
front door straight out the back door. The rooms
were on the side of the hallway that went from
front to back. There were no closets to hang
clothes, just a hook on the back of the door. Every
room including the living room had a bed.

After mom got over the shock of Coleman's
Alley, they settled down for the night. Her sister-
in-laws picked all through her suitcase wondering
what was brought for them. Then they looked
through her clothes and asked a thousand questions
of what it's like up north. She could have given
them anything, a book of matches from Horn and
Hardhart was a big deal. Of course the constant
marvel was her accent. To them, she talked funny.
They were full of questions and dreams of
escaping the south.

Although there were no street lights, black
out shades were pulled down every night. Mom

rolled around in the lumpy bed without the luxury of two clean sheets listening to who knows what kind of critter scratching under the house all night long. The next day mom went with her mother-in-law, Miss Ethel for a ride uptown.

Now I told you this was mid-July, a Carolina July. Mom got washed in a bathroom that was just to the side of the kitchen and had no door, just a curtain. Can you imagine? Imagine sitting in the kitchen eating eggs while someone is taking a shit behind a curtain. She got dressed and put on one of her cute little short sets. Her mother-in-law was rocking in the big chair on the porch and took notice of mom's scandalous attire.

"You gwine uptown looking that? A married woman. All your legs and stuff hanging out like that. You should put some clothes on!"

You got too many babies by too many men to worry about what I wear, mom thought to herself. She didn't care. To the shock of the entire family, she wore her shorts. Momma Lou flowed like fire through her veins.

They caught the bus on Pine Street to uptown Durham. Miss Ethel was mom's guide. They paid their fare in the front, got off and re-entered through the back door. It was the first time mom ever saw a White Only sign.

I believe we got off on Main Street. Coloreds were cordial but careful. They walked up and down the street eating their lunch. I never saw such a thing in my life. The white folks were nice enough.

Nobody said anything to me. Miss Ethel was careful to step aside when a white person walked by and never ever looked them in the eye. She always looked up, down or away. We walked in the clothing store and looked around. A white saleslady walked up on us—you know how they do.

"Canna hep ya please?"

"Size 18 dress ma'am?" Miss Ethel never looked at her.

"They rat down yonder."

"Yes ma'am." Miss Ethel looked down.

I just stood there and looked at the lady. She talked so flat. Miss Ethel snatched my arm to stop me from staring and to go with her. Coloreds couldn't try anything on—hats, shoes, nothing. It was peaceful, but tense.

Miss Ethel was up early to fix breakfast and start house work before the sun got too high. Mom offered to help with the laundry. She grabbed a basket and headed out the back door and met a beady red eyed snake in the woodpile. The fork tongue was the last straw. Mom's screams brought Miss Ethel out. She grabbed the axe nearby and chopped the head off. Without a word between them, she went back to the kitchen floor. Mom nervously finished hanging clothes as quickly as she could and returned inside. Miss Ethel had moved everything out of the kitchen, splashed up the floor with buckets of water then swept it out of the back door. Mom stood well out of the way watching soapless water splash onto the clothes she just hung up. By noon, it was too hot to move. They sat in the shade of the front porch all afternoon meeting with everyone who passed by. Miss Ethel finally got up to check on the pots. Dinner was served on tin plates that sat on a metal table. A pot of meat and green beans, called snaps, with biscuits was dinner washed down with a jar of water. They only went as far as the front porch and warned mom to stay close. Moths fluttered around a lonely naked bulb while Miss Ethel slowly rocked in her wicker chair catching the heavy night air. The family sat on around talking about much of nothing until bedtime. Without television, radio or phone to break the nothingness, mom longed for home well before her weeks' stay was over. The bus ride back home was not as exciting as the ride down. In fact, it took twice as long.

    The next time mom and dad went to Durham, they had that Chevy. Dad wanted to take mom for a ride to see the beautiful countryside. They drove pass Duke University toward the outskirts of Durham. It was the first time she ever saw Magnolia trees, sugar cane and cotton. She knew the difference between tobacco and collards leaves. They pulled into the colored end of the park for a rest. Mom came out from the colored bathroom and walked toward the water fountains behind a man who was walking his dog. She saw the white man take a drink from the white fountain then turned the knob on the colored fountain so his dog could get a drink. Mom wasn't thirsty anymore, just disgusted. As they continued their stroll, she came upon the sweetest looking watermelon along the side of the road where a trucker had his display. Since she didn't get that water, she thought this would do the trick. She walked up to the white huckster. While she approached, he said "Step right up nigger! Pick anyone you want. Only fifteen cents nigger, help yourself." It wasn't that mom never experienced nasty white folk; even in Gwynedd there were plenty of ugly people. She wasn't used to the brazenness of it. She was used to the quiet, sneaky white folks up north. She went right back in the car with no watermelon.

Bennie take me home! Now! I shouted. He was used to it, I wasn't. I had never seen such blatant disregard. I wasn't angry, I think I was confused. I never met Jim Crow before. Bastard.

When night time came, Pokey, Buttercup and Uncle Leroy loved to jump in the car and take mom to a couple of juke joints on the colored side of town. They liked to show off in front of their friends rolling up in a big car with Pennsylvania plates. Sometimes they took mom to Haiti, pronounced hay-tie. It was a little dirt town not worth the gas it took to drive there. They jumped in the car and went way down a dark dirt road to a worn out shell of a building with a ten watt bulb straining at the door.

They were some rough looking scoundrels in

*there. They looked like they just came off the field.
It had wooden tables and a dirt floor. Some little
beer band bounced in the corner and jelly jars
were full of corn liquor. I stayed close to Buttercup.
The Stallion Club in Emery Woods wasn't much
better. I brought a jug of liquor with me from the
A.B.C store. I poured a drink and put the bottle on
the table. Buttercup had a fit.*

*"NOOOO!!!" He shouted. "You got to keep
the bottle under the table. This is a dry state." he
warned.*

Now check this out. Dry state law states that
no liquor bottles are allowed on top of the table,
but you can have the glass you poured it in on the
table. The Klan, cops and law makers were all the
same crop who made, broke and enforced the law.
That same night a woman ran out of the bathroom
like someone chased her. She upset everything.
Mom didn't know whether to hide or run. The
place had just gotten the chain flush toilets and it
scared the woman to death. It was the first time she
ever saw a toilet flush. She was afraid she would
go down with the water. She wanted to go to the
outhouse or in the woods. Mom was again never so
glad to get back home.

I was old enough to remember when the
streets were paved in the mid to late sixties. I also
remember pulling to the side of the road to rest and
eat. I didn't know it was because we couldn't go
into the restaurants. If it wasn't for chicken and
potato salad, most of us would have starved to

death.

*I didn't understand how Jim Crow worked.
At that time, black people had to act dumb and
stay dumb to stay alive. They weren't allowed to
have anything decent, not even a mind. White folks
could just haul off and beat the shit out of any
colored man or woman. If coloreds fought back,
they could be killed or at least put in jail. If a black
man happened to look up and his eyes met with a
white woman, he was a rapist who had to be dealt
with. Tiny little towns like Dumfries or Dinwiddie
Virginia were no place to be somebody after dark
with out of state license and colored. Family
members of other people turned up missing. No
one dare asked. An aunt of yours was raped by a
white mob. She was accosted while walking down
the road during the day on her way home. She
later committed suicide. It was never spoken very
much. She was quietly buried and the family went
on with their daily lives, crying in their private
misery. Colored females were women and couldn't
be raped, but white females were vulnerable
ladies. Later I learned that a lot of white folks
knew Jim Crow was wrong, but they couldn't say
anything. Some sneaked and lied to help coloreds
as much as they could without risk of swinging
from a tree themselves.*

Pockets of people hadn't heard of some of
the popular jazz music and musicians in the dance
halls and on the radios. Many people were too poor

to have a radio or go to the dances and sponsors mostly catered to white musicians. There were two kinds of radio, gospel and country western. People didn't get around much. They were born, married, had children, and died in the same town. There just wasn't that much to know.

Broad, Leigh and Diamond Street homes were majestic. They were five and six bedroom houses with marble steps and brass hardware on the doors. Large airy rooms had beautiful hardwood floors, deep rich mahogany baseboards—stone fireplaces complemented quaint mosaic tile and statuesque oak banisters that journeyed to the third floor—the servants' quarters. Coloreds lived on smaller streets. Some homes had as few as four rooms.

After WWII, many of the white folks left Philly and moved to Levittown. The government built highways to neighborhoods for white folks only. They didn't even want Jews. Some sold their houses in North Philly, but others broke the houses into apartments and were some of our first slumlords. Jamming forty some odd people into these new apartments and they only came around to collect the rent but they didn't keep the places up.

Mom remembered as I drove her down Ridge Avenue.

On the other hand, they grew tired of making repairs time and again because too many

*people let the children do to suit themselves. Tons
of people piled into these houses with way too
many children for the cramped quarters flushing
toilet paper and bar soap down the toilet. Saturday
night drunks started fussin and fightin destroying
walls and fixtures—doors didn't close flush and
clothes pins were used to keep the oven door and
freezer door closed. Their places were loaded
down with weak chair legs, broken lamps and
busted sofa springs. Everybody was poor and the
white folks didn't do right, but it didn't call for all
of that. It was the first time I saw trifling with my
own eyes.*

    *The Ridge was jumping. I must admit, it was
a good time—too good to miss. But too many
people were starting to get out of hand. I
remember when I was child, people were coming
up from down the road with nothing and tucked in
with family. They fussed and fought and worked to
keep everybody fed until they could go out on their
own. When I came to the city, plenty of colored
people worked and struggled to have decent lives
and make a future for their children. But
somewhere along the line, a crop of destructive
Negroes started to spoil it for everybody. I don't
think anybody knows where they came from, but it
prompted the start of those who could to move out.*

    When rent included utilities, people cooked
for everyone they knew, turkeys and pies everyday
all day long. By the sixties, these properties were

being abandoned by their owners and later became uninhabitable shells after the riots. Women for the most part didn't know anything about child support or spousal support. Even if they did it would be like trying to get blood from a stone. Opportunities for black women to get an education and a decent job were still difficult to come by for the masses. Welfare wasn't as prevalent as many thought it was. Hustling paid the bills. Women ran houses of food, liquor and gambling. Other women used the gold mine they sat on to feed the kids. Some stayed quietly in the house while others pranced in church or the bar—whoever had the money to feed the kids was their new source of income which unfortunately made more kids. For women who made good money, the good life was waiting.

Mom was watching her brand new television from Gimbels department store. She loved the show *Gangbusters* when it was on the radio, now a television program. Afterward she saw a news report showing a beautiful woman being arrested for disobedience. It was Missus Rosa Parks. It was in all of the papers and big talk in the neighborhood. There was a lot of nervous talk going on. That was when North Philly started to turn and the great exodus began.

Everyone felt it, but nobody knew what it was. Something was changing. The paper had stories about the boycott. Kids were going to jail. Don't forget, we were all still pissed about Emmett

Till. I saw that picture in Jet Magazine—everybody saw it and I don't think colored folks been right since. That's what really started the Movement if you ask me. Then the riots started trying to get those children into school in Little Rock. Up here, Cecil B. Moore was rising up. With a fifth of Old Grand Dad and a cigar he raised hell all over the city and burned ears with the funky truth. He led the NAACP Philadelphia Chapter, stopped The Mummers from using blackface, knocked down the walls of Girard College and integrated the union. He was rough around the edges but was exactly what we needed then—and now. The Tribune, we called it the Black Dispatch, was filled with the latest. Pace Alexander was an up and coming lawyer. He represented a young woman, Coreen Sykes. She was the first black woman in this state to go to the chair. At the same time, black society was getting big. Some coloreds were getting smooth and classy.

Professional people began to leave North Philly for Lincoln Drive or Germantown. Middle class Negroes were moving on and a polarization was more noticeable.

Aunt Nettie was hanging her wash in the back and mom zipped out of the front door to Ridge Avenue to shop. With her market cart in hand, she enjoyed strolling the avenue, meeting and greeting people while getting her groceries, barely noticing the flashing lights blaring sirens. As she turned the corner to come home she stopped dead in her tracks looking at lights in front of her house. She almost upset her groceries getting in the house.

I was so upset. I asked Uncle Will what happened. He said "I was looking for Nettie. I kept calling her and I fell over her body in the yard."

She was gone. I was devastated. Aunt Nettie had been so good to me, almost like a mother and now she's gone.

The year 1959 rolled around. The Earle Theater was gone and the neighborhood was changing. Mom and dad finally got their wish. They were able to move out of that third floor apartment and into their own home. They moved to Cobbs Creek Park in West Philly. From that home they had me, a big band, local notoriety and acquired a wealth of knowledge that no university can hope to teach. They were on a roll and so were the good times.

As soon as I was grown I wanted to get out in the world. There were too many new things going on; disco, computers, school, men, my home girls, money and enjoying life. Then something happened. During the early to mid eighties, I didn't like what was going on. I began to lose interest in television and didn't understand the music. It didn't entertain me— I couldn't feel it in the way I used to. What didn't annoy me put me to sleep. Boredom slowly crept into my soul disturbing my disposition in ways of which I was not aware. Had I been without my roots, experts would have prescribed a pill for sure. An insidious force began to erode daily life. Repetitious conversations were filled with nothing, just hollow groups of words all day long. Politically correct just came to town and censored the shit out of everything. Violence seemed to increase without even a vague agenda of avengement like the sixties. The night clubs I used to haunt were either gone or were a victim of violence.

The evening news was filled with lost whales, a distraught teenager who couldn't find the right prom gown, the latest gossip on amateur shows and the soap saga of a celebrity couple or maybe a face painting carnival in a sleepy town. Options slowly disappeared; what to like, what to eat, what to do and for how long. There were more one sided arguments. Medication became the solution to everything. People went from protesting and politicking to purchasing. I saw a confused, well educated, sleep deprived populace that ran through red lights and sat at green ones while having the nerve to be hell bent on saving me from myself. What seemed to be clearly understood and valued as common sense less than a decade ago was now lost on everyone complicating every issue from having dinner to how to cook it.

Improvisation is the key to survival where the new world dictates otherwise. Reflection for me creates solace, knowledge and strength that totally invalidate most new age information which changes all the time leaving one floundering for solid ground. I needed freedom from our dysfunctional culture— a culture that systematically destroys mobility and cultivates confusion and ignorance—for our own good. Of course.

I had to go. Had to go home. I needed the roots I so furiously ran from in my youth. I needed that old school where the truth never changes, only lies. The truth is never forgotten or manipulated. It is as reliable as the moon and the sun.

I awoke to a beautiful Tuesday morning in April and before my foot hit the floor I couldn't wait for the day to be over. I was in no mood for boredom and bullshit today. So I called in sick. I felt much better. Then I called my mother who was anxious to break out. She was ready to throw the television out the window. That's when it hit me. I packed my bag— tax papers from 1930s and pictures of Sunday dinners from long ago.

"Mom how would you like to see the old house today?" I felt like I had the world on a string.

"Yea, let's take a ride."

We hit Bethlehem Pike all the way up. Mom pointed out just about every house; who lived there, who worked there, the old school house. We turned left onto Sunmeytown Pike.

"See that house back there? That's where young girls got rid of their babies. Never saw anybody go in or come out. Still looks empty don't it? Turn right here for a minute."

I followed what she said.

"Now turn up this road."

"You mean Meetinghouse Road?"

"Yea. This used to be Cowpath Road. Me and Dorothy came up this road many a day to old Hollingsworth Farm. All of this was field loaded down with berries. Lawd looka here! Nothin but drywall developments now."

On my left was the old farm now Sleepy Hollow Farm.

"That's where Aunt Nina and Uncle Lush worked. Back over in those woods was where those night doctors used to be. It was some kinda black dark and lonely up here."

I turned around the back way to come south on Route 202, turned left onto Sumneytown, then to Swedesford Road. There it was and it was more beautiful than ever.

I drove up to the edge of the driveway. A petite woman was trimming hedges with a young girl and a yapping dog that seemed to defy our presence. A salt and pepper haired man was in the yard fiddling with some type of outdoorsy contraption. I got out of the car and gently introduced myself to her.

"Oh you're Joe Williams' cousin!" she pleasantly smiled.

"Yes, my mother and I wanted to see the old house if it's alright." They turned the old house into a palace. It was absolutely beautiful! I showed the missus some of the old pictures and tax papers. She and her husband invited us both inside. They were most welcoming.

I took mom in the house to the room where she was born. After I explained to the Drumms the history of that room, nobody said anything for a moment. Even the dog stopped yapping. I stood still in the same as I had done more than forty years ago. Never thought I'd see the day.

The Drumms let us wonder the grounds alone. I suppose they knew this was something special for us. More than eighty years old, mom is a bit frail and tires easily. Her robust spirit encased in her feeble body needed a little help to where the old barn used to be. I tried to imagine the field when there were chickens running around and fruits and vegetables flourished and the air was filled with the aroma of flowers and spices cut by the occasional stench from pigs and manure. I tried to see the little chicks and kittens clumsily prancing around while the piglets fought to suckle their mother. I envisioned bright white clothes blowing in the gentle breeze while another load was slowly boiling clean in the tub and children were picking the crop of the day for dinner. The memory lingered so long and loud for mom that soon I felt it too. I saw it as if we were there— together, as if we were both remembering that time. The apple and pear trees were still there but their yield was small. I pulled an apple from that tree— the same tree from which mommy had, Nana had and Momma Lou had—the same tree. I took a bite of the hard and bitter apple but I didn't taste it with my mouth. It was through my mother's heart, her nostalgia that I tasted all of her bittersweet memories that are now baptized into my soul. She reached for my apple and had a bite too. It confirmed our personal communion that made many moments at the old house more than special. It's a big feeling, a deep moment with a lot of love and history.

Momma Lou died nineteen years before my birth but not even death could keep me from knowing her. Mom kept her alive in my life. I know what she liked, how she dressed, the food she ate and how hard she worked and prayed. I heard about her pain and her struggle. I know all about her except the sound of her voice. So when I bite that apple she is somehow in the core—a core filled with the sorrow of slavery—filled with wisdom and strength. Its aftertaste leaves the divine question of what is it all about?

That apple tree has endured many storms. Through the hottest summer and most brutal winter, it managed to bear shade leaves and fruit for knowledge. Just like life for the rest of us it has had years of abundance and shortage. It caught the fire of lightning and dealt with the death of leaves and limbs. It provided a home for birds and squirrels and none of this would be possible without nourishment from mother earth, the start and end of us all. The dark rich soil momma said looked like chocolate isn't as pure as it used to be. Modern days have undermined, dare I say disrespected the art of nurture and time especially time necessary for wholesome growth. A cozy fire will be the final deed for that tree one day, but for almost one hundred years it nurtured life and for mom and me on this day, it nurtured us.

We didn't talk but the firm hold she had on my arm gave me a sense her memories were comforting her. The memory of pies, cider and jelly her grandmother made from those apples and the fun she had climbing its limbs. It's been sixty some odd years since she sought that tree for nourishment. She wanted me to get another apple from the high limb this time, as her grandmother always told her.

That tree was Momma Lou's touchstone and

she was the only somebody who ever really loved my mother. Somewhere between hope and despair mom survived and embraced life. It was Luella who created that space in my mother's being to love, learn and teach. It is that space we share in comfort with her— a timeless gift that came from that tree— the physical root to my soul. Mom stood on the ground where she started. We walked through the field where grass and weeds have hidden Momma Lou's sweat and toil. All that I am and know came from her and that tree. When I visit her grave she touches my soul. Her liaison is her granddaughter who was her love and mine too.

CPSIA information can be obtained
at www.ICGtesting.com
Printed in the USA
BVHW031825180620
581847BV00001B/96